Soviet Aims in Central America

Soviet Aims in Central America

THE CASE OF NICARAGUA

G. W. Sand

Foreword by Lewis A. Tambs

PRAEGER

New York
Westport, Connecticut
London

Library of Congress Cataloging-in-Publication Data

Sand, G. W. (Gregory W.)
    Soviet aims in Central America : the case of Nicaragua / G.W. Sand ;
    foreword by Lewis A. Tambs.
        p.   cm.
    Bibliography: p.
    Includes index.
    ISBN 0–275–93050–5 (alk. paper)
    1. Soviet Union—Foreign relations—Nicaragua.   2. Nicaragua—
Foreign relations—Soviet Union.   3. Nicaragua—Foreign
relations—1979–   I. Title.
DK69.3.N5S26   1989
327.4707285—dc20   89-33959

Copyright © 1989 by G.W. Sand

Library of Congress Catalog Card Number : 89–33959
ISBN: 0–275–93050–5

First published in 1989

Praeger Publishers, One Madison Avenue, New York, NY 10010
A division of Greenwood Press, Inc.

Printed in the United States of America

The paper used in this book complies with the
Permanent Paper Standard issued by the National
Information Standards Organization (Z39.48–1984).

10 9 8 7 6 5 4 3 2 1

Contents

Foreword

Lewis A. Tambs

The United States has enjoyed unprecedented security on both its southern and northern frontiers since 1867. Not since the fall of the French-supported Mexican empire of Maximilian and the removal of the Czarist threat by the purchase of Russian-America along with the establishment of the Dominion of Canada has this country been obliged to contend with the possibility of overland invasion. Two years later, by completing the transcontinental railroad in 1869, the United States freed itself from complete dependence on its sea-lanes of communications between the Atlantic and Pacific coasts around Cape Horn or the sea and land routes through the Caribbean and the Panamanian, Nicaraguan, or Mexican passages to the Pacific.

Thus, by 1869, friendly neighbors and vast deserts shielded the south, while increasing Anglo-American understanding protected the north. Additionally, railroads outflanked sea power in the intercoastal continental trade.

No previous power—Babylon, Persia, Egypt, Rome, China, the Caliphate, Portugal, Spain, France, Germany, or Russia—has ever had such an advantageous strategic situation. Only Japan and Great

Britain were partially protected by their moats, but both were threatened time and again by seaborne armies from Eurasia. They were guarded by straits and channels; the United States, by the Atlantic and Pacific.

Acquisitions of naval bases in the Caribbean and construction of the Trans-Isthmian Canal further strengthened U.S. security. As U.S. influence expanded into the Caribbean basin after 1898, replacing Britain in the New World Mediterranean, the closed sea of the Caribbean and Central America emerged as the perch of U.S. global power. In two world wars the ability of the United States to project power eastward across the Atlantic to Europe and the Middle East, and westward across the Pacific to Asia, was based on a cooperative Caribbean basin and a supportive South America. Not since the Spanish-American War has the United States been obliged to commit massive resources of men, money, or matériel southward. Not so anymore.

Soviet satellization of Cuba, with its continued commitment to exporting Wars of National Liberation and the establishment of a Marxist-Leninist base on the mainland of North America in Nicaragua, has altered the idyllic equation. The U.S. sanctuary, as Dr. G. W. Sand so admirably details in the following pages, is now open to the south. For the Sandinista slogan of *Revolución sin fronteras* (Revolution without Frontiers) reveals their tactics; and the third stanza of the "Sandinista Hymn," which declares that the "Yankees are the enemy of Humanity," indicates their ultimate objective—the United States of America.

The immediate threat is not, however, armed assault, but destabilization of U.S. society by millions of revolution-driven refugees seeking safety north of the Rio Grande—Operation Checkmate—a scenario which envisions the United States either withdrawing to Fortress America to shield its southern flank or being overrun by innocent insurgent-driven exiles. This possibility of an ancient ground game—which the nuclear balance of terror has made feasible—along with the Soviet's two other major strategic maneuvers—to surround the People's Republic of China and deprive the Western industrialized nations of access to the oil of the Middle

East and the minerals of southern Africa—add weight to the following exposition. Dr. Sand has presented an accurate account of the end of an era, whereby the United States, secure on its southern and northern flanks, could devote its attention and energy to the Atlantic and Pacific sea frontiers.

Acknowledgments

This analysis is based on key documents, on important secondary sources, and on the help of many individuals: participants in the immediate "target area," U.S. officials, scholars both in the United States and abroad, librarians who have given of their time and effort, and my graduate students on Central America and in other of my courses on International Relations, whose lively interest and research have aided my own.

In particular, I owe a special thanks to Dr. Alejandro Bolaños Geyer, whose generous help and guidance through the thicket of Nicaragua's sometimes tortured past has been unfailing, and to Dr. Lewis A. Tambs, formerly U.S. ambassador to Costa Rica (1985–87) and Colombia (1983–85). Also, Dr. Oscar Sevilla Sacasa, Nicaragua's foreign minister during the 1950s, has helped in providing some new information on Fidel Castro and on Quintín Pino Machado. Others who have helped in various and sundry ways include Dr. Peter Clement, Brian Crozier, Georgie Anne Geyer, Lawrence E. Harrison, Professors Joseph Kalvoda and Wolfgang Leonhard, Stanislav Levchenko, Professor John Norton Moore, Douglas Payne, Herbert Romerstein, Sol Sanders, and

Amanda Velázquez. Lastly, to Karen Luebbert and the staff of the Eden-Webster Libraries, who provided for my research needs and office space, I am truly indebted; and to Bill Olbrich of Washington University and John Waide of Saint Louis University, in lightening my research needs, I am twice indebted. Above all, to my wife Jane, without whose encouragement this book may not have been written, I owe my unbounded gratitude.

Soviet Aims in Central America

Introduction: The Americas, Soviet Strategy, and World War III

THE AMERICAS AND WORLD WAR III

In 1947, a conference of the Communist parties of the Soviet Union, Bulgaria, Czechoslovakia, Hungary, Poland, Rumania, and Yugoslavia, including the Communist parties of France and Italy, was held in Silesia between September 22–27, at which the Communist Information Bureau, or Cominform, was founded. The Cominform was not important in itself; its last formal meeting took place in November 1949, but it was important as a symbol. It represented Stalin's formal declaration of political warfare against the West. Thus, in a symbolic sense, it represented the start of World War III.[1] Indeed, within weeks of that historic meeting the world Communist parties were ordered to place themselves in the vanguard of the opposition to Western imperialism, inciting militant opposition and general strikes in Western Europe and Latin America, most notably, as it turned out, in the Communist-led riots in Bogotá, Colombia, in April 1948.

Less than three years after the end of World War II, the near destruction of Bogotá was indicative of the long-term threat that

Stalin's Silesian initiative posed to Western interests and Western security in general. In retrospect, the Soviet-inspired plan to scuttle the Ninth Inter-American Conference meeting in Bogotá was symbolic in another sense. It brought the name of one Fidel Castro, then only 21, to the attention of conference delegates. Castro, who was in Bogotá as a Cuban delegate to the International Communist Youth Congress also meeting then, was acting on orders of the Soviet Embassy in Havana (the Soviet Union did not break diplomatic relations with Cuba until 1952) "to interrupt" the proceedings of the Inter-American Conference of Foreign Ministers, using whatever means necessary, including violence.[2] Eyewitness accounts of the destruction in Bogotá alone, on April 9–10, 1948, can hardly be exaggerated. Some 150 buildings were destroyed, resulting in 500 deaths. A U.S. Foreign Service officer on the scene, Cecil B. Lyon, estimated the damage in Bogotá to be equal to the property damage caused throughout Colombia: about $300 million.[3] In 1960, before a Senate subcommittee to hear testimony on the Communist threat to the United States throughout the Caribbean, former U.S. Ambassador to Brazil William D. Pawley, then a member of that delegation, testified that he and another delegate distinctly recalled the voice over the radio, stating that a "Communist revolution" was in progress, that the president of Colombia had been killed, and that the national army had capitulated. The speaker announced himself as "Fidel Castro from Cuba," Pawley recalled.[4]

The *Bogotazo*, as the event came to be called, may in fact have helped to bring the twenty-one American states closer together on issues affecting their common security. George C. Marshall, for example, who headed the U.S. delegation, had been instrumental in quelling fears of Communist threats among the delegates. The conference thus stayed its course, replacing the Pan-American Union with the new Organization of American States as a regional organization within the framework of the United Nations Charter. A new council replaced the old governing board of the Union, along with a Joint Military Staff and an Economic and Social Council. As Marshall's biographer noted: "Events in Bogotá had helped rather than hurt the United States, since the conviction that the Communists had at least a hand in the uprising had aided the passage of antitotalitarian resolutions."[5]

Despite Stalin's failure to derail the Bogotá meeting of American states, that failure was more than offset by the "national front" strategy which brought Czechoslovakia into the Soviet camp in 1948, an event in turn that helped fuel Soviet ambitions anew, especially in Latin America. The addition of Czechoslovakia to the Soviet bloc represented an important industrial and foreign-policy gain for Soviet policy, with the pivot state of the "heartland" now in virtual control of all of Eastern and Central Europe. Stalin lost little time in creating an institution in Prague to help train future revolutionaries in Latin America. Indeed, the new center for training a professional revolutionary elite in the Czech capital was named the Graduate School of Latin American Studies.[6] Beginning in the 1950s, other such schools were established, as well as training camps for Third World revolutionaries in the Soviet Union itself, at Simferopol, Baku, Tashkent, and Odessa. Enormous sums were spent in this way for training and indoctrination in Communist ideology, and in the techniques of guerrilla warfare. Raúl Castro, brother of Fidel Castro, who graduated from the Prague School in the early 1950s, would learn how to manipulate keywords and phrases, disguise his Communist affiliation, and handle firearms, drugs, and poison.[7]

By the early 1950s, the Castro brothers had again surfaced in Cuban public life. Following their failed attempt to incite an insurrection against the Batista regime, by staging an attack on an army post in Santiago de Cuba in 1953, the incident was important in that it focused attention on the nascent ideas of Castro's political movement. What the 26th of July Movement intended could not have been more apparent than from the speech given by Castro in his own defense, though not from the pamphlet later published as his defense. In the speech at his trial, he opposed the very notion of democratic government. He called instead for "revolutionary laws," stating that if his rebel movement had succeeded in bringing him to power, he would have nullified Cuba's constitution by

placing all legislative, executive, and judicial power in the hands
of the revolutionary movement. The judiciary would have been
abolished and replaced by "Special Courts." Such courts would
have been empowered "to confiscate all holdings and ill-gotten
gains," a blank check for any and all confiscations. Castro even
falsely argued that the Cuban people had been the victims of
capitalist exploitation, another indication that any and all foreign-
owned property would likewise have been confiscated.[8] Subsequently, though Castro and other survivors of the 26th of July
Movement were sentenced to fifteen years in the Isle of Pines
prison, the Batista regime, besieged by pleas of clemency, amnes-
tied the survivors, including the Castro brothers, in May 1955.

Oddly, for the period from mid–1955 to January 1959, scholarly
accounts have tended to neglect the extent of Soviet and Soviet
bloc involvement in Castro's rise to power. Such evidence as the
relative affluence of the Latin American Communist parties, as
compared to the less affluent, and the need of a "front man" at the
head of an insurgent movement, should have alerted officials to
the likely existence of a "regular subsidy," let alone the inference,
as Carlos Rangel noted, that Stalin had discovered the "soft underbelly" of the United States in Latin America.[9]

Though exiled in Mexico, Castro and his followers engaged in
activities that did not escape the attention of the Nicaraguan
ambassador in Mexico City, Alejandro Arguello Montiel, nor of
the U.S. ambassador in Havana, Arthur Gardner. So dangerous did
Castro appear to be to Batista, that Ambassador Arguello Montiel
notified Nicaragua's foreign minister, Dr. Oscar Sevilla Sacasa, of
the threat posed by Castro's rebel army, then regrouping at a ranch
in Mexico. Sevilla Sacasa subsequently traveled to Cuba to meet
with Batista concerning the Castro issue. But Batista apparently
was not interested in exchanging intelligence reports on the activities or plans of Fidel Castro. So Sevilla Sacasa's initiative was
abandoned through lack of interest on Batista's part.[10]

Still, Castro's activities did not go unreported. Interested diplomatic and military personnel stationed in Mexico City learned of
the growing numbers of Castro's guerrillas, including Ernesto

"Che" Guevara, who had come from Guatemala, and of Major Alberto Bayo, who had served on the Republican side in the Spanish Civil War. Bayo, in fact, would be instrumental in training members of Castro's rebel army in Mexico and later in Oriente Province in Cuba.

The precedent of dispatching arms to promote subversion in Latin America had earlier been established in Guatemala, when Czech arms were delivered to the Arbenz regime on the Swedish vessel the *Alfhem*.[11] Similarly, in 1955, only a year after the overthrow of the Arbenz regime in Guatemala, the Castro brothers established contact with the Czech commercial attaché for the purpose of obtaining arms, including financial assistance provided through the Soviet Embassy in Mexico City. Colonel Andrés Pérez-Chaumont, Cuba's military attaché in Mexico City, later testified on the Soviet and Czech links with the Castro movement in Mexico.[12] Following Castro's landfall on Cuban soil in December 1956, others would also testify on the Soviet resupply of Castro's forces in the Sierra Maestra, notably by submarine.[13] Yet even this clandestine effort may have failed, if the United States had not imposed an arms embargo on Cuba, a signal that the United States favored a successor regime to that of President Batista. The fateful decision of March 1958, when the Eisenhower administration suspended the supply of war matériel to Batista, was not unlike the scene some twenty years later, when the Carter administration suspended arms shipments to President Somoza of Nicaragua, a decision that likewise played into the hands of the Sandinistas and their supporters, the Soviet Union, and Cuba.[14]

Juan Vives has well stated the problem in his book, *The Masters of Cuba*, when he concluded, after being near the elite of Cuban power as an intelligence agent for many years, that Fidel Castro has been a Soviet agent since the late 1940s. He wondered, moreover, "if Allen Dulles, who directed the CIA when Castro took power had foreseen this possibility. The fact is," he added, "that a Communist became a head of government ninety miles from the United States, with the apparent ignorance of the CIA."[15]

The Americas in Soviet Strategy

Ideological and political warfare was an established tradition in Soviet foreign policy when Nikita Khrushchev ended the Cominform policy of 1947 by recasting it, in 1956, under the mantle of "peaceful coexistence." The new initiative signaled only that the future of East-West conflict need not end in a general war. Yet that initiative suggested an even greater threat than Stalin's more openly hostile "two camps" policy, since it emphasized the Soviet commitment (by 1961) to support so-called wars of national liberation in Asia, Africa, and Latin America. Soviet foreign policy would now combine the principles of peaceful coexistence and expansion, using "the first to camouflage the second."[16] To implement that strategy by attacking imperialism through its "weakest link" in Latin America, including the aim of the Latin American Communist parties of encircling the United States, the Kremlin's united or national-front strategy raised the specter of insurgent warfare being waged in the Americas and against the Americas itself.

Such an insurgency had almost taken place nearly two years before Khrushchev's announced policy statement on coexistence. The failure to install a radical regime then was mainly faulted on the failure to neutralize Guatemala's National Army.[17] Indeed, Khrushchev had been taught a valuable lesson by that failure, as had Castro himself. But equally important, as it turned out, was the lesson of protracted guerrilla warfare in helping to demoralize civilian authority at home as well as in deceiving those in civilian authority abroad.

Expert opinion, in congressional hearings conducted on the Communist threat throughout the Caribbean between 1959 and 1971, held that the Soviets planned and took control of Cuba for one basic reason: for the stated purpose of worldwide subversion against the "target area" (the non-Communist world), and against the United States in particular as the leading state in the non-Communist world. But it was not until the Tricontinental Conference of 1966 in Havana (examined in the next chapter) that the Soviets managed to promote their principal goal of exploring opportunities for other Vietnam-type wars, and for creating a centralized entity expressly for that purpose. The Havana Conference, moreover, marked the culmination of more than five years of Soviet preparation in seeking to consolidate their military and political control over Cuba so as to acquire a formal base for subversion in the region and beyond.[18]

Moscow's geostrategic ambitions were thus fueled by the overthrow of the Batista regime in Cuba, as can be inferred from numerous official Soviet statements on geopolitics. Perhaps no one has stated these ambitions in more sweeping terms than the former head of the Soviet navy, Admiral Sergei G. Gorshkov. "He who controls the sea controls world commerce, and he who controls world commerce controls the resources of the earth, and the earth itself," he stated, adding that "the goal of Soviet sea power is to effectively utilize the world ocean in the interests of building world communism."[19] Hence Soviet control over Cuba greatly extended the potential range of Soviet air and sea power beyond the Eurasian landmass. Indeed, by 1959, the Soviets had found their way to the Atlantic approaches of the Panama Canal and the "soft underbelly" of the U.S. Gulf Coast.[20]

Since the Soviets believe that the bulk of the world's unexploited natural resources lie along the rimlands of the Pacific basin, it must be assumed that they are planning to target these same rimland states, much as they regard the Pacific itself as the ocean of the future. Likewise, since the Soviet program of maritime expansion represents a vital state interest and is essential to maritime supremacy, they must seek to achieve oceanic and rimland hegemony in the Americas.[21] But in order to achieve such mastery and the complementary aim of encircling the United States, they must first gain a foothold in Central America, as they already have in Cuba, thereby extending their influence both northward to Mexico and southward to the Panama Canal.

It is why the issue of control and who rules in Central America today is so important to the future of the Americas. The Soviet leaders will not challenge the United States where it is strongest, as it was in the Caribbean in 1962, but they will not cease to challenge North America where they find weakness and lack of resolve. If the United States should be unwilling to keep Central America in the Western world, it stands to lose not only its natural allies, the other "sea peoples" of the world, but also World War III, which has now long been in progress.

Nonetheless, the Soviet system, despite its outward strength, is inwardly at odds with itself. Though the subject of ideology is briefly examined in relation to Soviet aims, it is essential to underscore the importance of ideology in understanding so unusual a threat. It is also essential to recognize that the Soviet leaders, the Party *nomenklatura*, cannot tolerate internal dissent, since an attack on official doctrine (Marxism-Leninism) is an assault on the Party itself. Neither can it permit external competition, because the continued existence of opposing philosophies poses a further threat to imperial unity. "Ideological empires," it has been said, "must strive for all or relapse into nothing."[22]

Lastly, this introduction would be incomplete if it did not include a brief comment on the paramount issue examined in this book. It concerns the outcome of a process that began with the Soviet incursion into the Western Hemisphere, beginning with its intervention in Cuba. Paul Bethel has given us the benefit of his vast knowledge on this aspect of Soviet aggression in the Americas in his important book, *The Losers*. But we have no similar study of the Soviets' subsequent aggression against Nicaragua, and now in progress against all of Central America. It is significant that the Soviets have gone out of their way to deny any involvement in bringing a Marxist-Leninist regime to power in Nicaragua. Even U.S. scholars have been assured by Kremlin officials that the Soviet government "had no contacts with the Sandinistas when they started their revolution," denying also that they had in any way "inspired it."[23] With few exceptions, both press and scholarly writings have failed to link the Soviets with the Sandinistas, a link that has been partially obscured by the "indigenous" character of the Nicaraguan Revolution. Nonetheless, in the following chapters the weight of evidence will show that Soviet denials of involve-

ment cannot stand up to scrutiny of the evidence in the case of
Nicaragua.

1

Nicaragua in
Soviet Foreign Policy,
1959–1979

SANDINISTA ORIGINS TO PANCASÁN

For the Soviet Union, Castro's victory had been an important lesson in strategic terms, in proving once again that Lenin's "double strategy" of supporting two Communist groups in the same country was sound strategy.[1] Similarly, since Castro's 26th of July Movement had been an opportunity in search of a revolution against a discredited regime, Castro knew that only the election of a liberal leader in 1958 stood in the way of his proximate plans of seizing power. It was not, to be sure, unlike the period some twenty years later, when the Sandinistas would also come to power, preceding the overthrow of another discredited regime in the region. And as Castro before them, the Sandinistas knew that deception was essential, since they could not afford to lose public support; hence it became equally important to obscure the question of support and political allegiances. As Paul Bethel has noted: "Communists do not join movements unless they have solid reason to expect a pay-off for their support."[2]

Indeed, that the Soviets would again attempt to gain a foothold in the Americas so soon after their failure in Guatemala raises profound questions as to the character and purpose of U.S. leadership and U.S.–Latin American policy. On the other hand, the circumstances surrounding Castro's rise to power in Cuba should have left few, if any, doubts in the minds of Washington officials as to the character and purpose of Soviet foreign policy. It was as though Nikita Khrushchev had told other party officials at the time that he did not intend to let Presidents Eisenhower and Somoza stop him the next time. (Somoza had financed and equipped Colonel Castillo Armas, enabling him to oust the Arbenz regime in Guatemala in 1954.) It was, in fact, just as the Cuban missile crisis was ending a few years later, that a long-time Soviet official used almost these exact words in warning John J. McCloy at the United Nations, admonishing him that "you Americans will never be able to do this to us again."[3]

Hence the Soviet initiative against Cuba worked in bringing Castro to power and in supporting his regime from the outset, despite the principle of geographic fatalism and, above all, the Monroe Doctrine. As Che Guevara boasted to one of Cuba's most respected lawyers shortly after being appointed to head the National Bank of Cuba: "The Castro regime and Yankee imperialism are engaged in a death struggle, and we both know that one of the two must die in this fight."[4]

For their part, the Soviets wasted little time after recognizing the new government, on January 10, 1959, in reestablishing de facto diplomatic relations between the two countries for the first time since 1952. In the same month, Aleksandr Alexeyev (real name Aleksandr I. Shitov) arrived in Cuba ostensibly as a TASS news correspondent to gather material for a feature story on Castro and Cuba's revolution. As a State Security (KGB) official, however, his real purpose was to conduct an intelligence survey in order to plan the establishment of Cuba's intelligence service. So useful was Alexeyev, that Castro requested he be appointed Soviet Ambassador to Cuba, a post he would hold until Moscow began to tighten its control over Cuba in 1967.[5] Moreover, next to the

Soviets' replacing Cuba's economic dependence on the United States, and their military commitment to Cuba in 1960, a principal focus of Soviet-Cuban policy before 1967 concerned the clandestine strategy of waging guerrilla warfare in the Americas. Indeed, Guevara as strategist and Alberto Bayo as guerrilla trainer were preoccupied with the aim of extending Cuba's liberationist war to the rest of Latin America.

Even as Castro was being sworn in as Cuba's prime minister in February 1959, Cubans and Nicaraguans were holding a meeting at the Habana Libre (formerly the Havana Hilton Hotel), where they publicly called for the overthrow of the Nicaraguan government. It was the first indication that Alberto Bayo was organizing expeditions against Cuba's Latin neighbors with that aim in view.[6] Several such expeditions were mounted to export Cuba's liberationist war to Nicaragua, Haiti, the Dominican Republic, and Panama. Rebuffed by these Guevarist-inspired efforts to promote revolution by force, Castro turned to methods of subversion in an effort to overthrow his hated rival in Nicaragua, President Luis Somoza. Accordingly, Castro appointed Quintín Pino Machado as his first ambassador to Nicaragua (and last under Somoza) in late 1959 or early 1960. In his short tenure as ambassador, Pino Machado succeeded in establishing an organization called Patriotic Youth. According to former Sandinistas, it was this student movement that gave rise to the future Sandinista Front, or FSLN, in power today in Nicaragua. The Cuban ambassador formed the Sandinistas, according to Fausto Amador, brother of the former FSLN leader Carlos Fonseca, adding that Cubans were the architects of the FSLN both in its construction and in choosing its leadership.[7]

Looking back, though Castro's and Guevara's early plans for exporting revolution failed, none would have been sustainable without the direct support of the Soviet bloc. Indeed, there was never any indication that the Soviet Union intended to abandon Cuba's "armed struggle" in promoting wars of national liberation in Latin America. To have adopted a contrary policy would have amounted to a renunciation of Marxism-Leninism and of the class struggle against so-called imperialism in the Americas. Similarly, for Castro to have even hinted that the "myth" about the backwardness of Latin America was not due mainly to North American imperialism would have been preposterous. Still, there were those, even in high places, who thought that U.S. provocation might cause Castro to turn to the Soviet Union. Consequently, friendliness toward Castro might cause him to abandon his armed struggle in favor of good relations, even with Cuba's Latin neighbors. So it was the greatest of ironies when these sentiments regarding adverse Sandinista actions again surfaced during President Carter's only term, lest the United States remain on the friendliest of terms with the new regime in Nicaragua.[8]

For anyone, then, who cared to learn from history, it seems odd that Moscow's clear intentions toward Cuba would have gone unnoticed by the beginning of 1960. In truth, April 1960 marked a kind of turning point for Cubans who still hoped to keep the Castro regime in the Western world. Yet such efforts were of no avail, as the first shipment of Soviet supplies reached Cuba under a Soviet-Cuban trade agreement signed in February of that year.[9] By December 1960, the Kremlin sought to dramatize its triumph by bringing together the largest assembly of Communist parties ever to meet at a conference in the Soviet capital. The conference was attended by some eighty-one Communist parties, and Khrushchev took the occasion to assert that "the victory of the Cuban revolution has powerfully stimulated the struggle of the Latin American peoples for complete national independence" in its "struggle against imperialism."[10] And in January 1961, Khrushchev again boasted before an assembly of party officials and academicians that Cuba's liberation provided "unlimited maneuverability" in the avoidance of world war in preference to "local wars." In short, since local wars were controllable, the field was wide open to the exploitation of indigenous forces in seizing the initiative against unpopular regimes, as Castro's liberation war had demonstrated.[11]

Thus was forged the Soviet-Cuban agency called the General

Directorate of Intelligence (DGI) in mid–1961 to organize and plan such initiatives. Its first director, Major Manuel Piñeiro Losada, headed its operations until 1969, when differences over strategy resulted in his reassignment and replacement by a protégé of Raúl Castro, José Méndez Cominches. Ultimately, however, the DGI came under direct Soviet supervision with the appointment of Viktor Simonov, a KGB colonel. Yet for Castro, as for Guevara until 1967, the continuation of armed struggle was his single most important interest in organizing the new intelligence service. Hence, of the eight departments of the DGI, the Department of National Liberation (LN), one of the largest, reflected Castro's ability to get his own way during this initial stage. The Liberation Directorate—as it came to be called—was divided into geographical sections for the Caribbean, Central America, and South America. Its function, as might be expected, was to plan guerrilla and other subversive acts and to provide logistical support for sending LN forces to the different regions.[12]

To be sure, Nicaragua occupied a special place on Fidel Castro's agenda for waging guerrilla warfare in Central America, partly because it was from that country that the U.S.-supported Cuban exiles launched their invasion of Cuba in 1961. From Castro's perspective, moreover, Nicaragua posed a security threat to the Cuban Revolution and to his own political survival. Consequently, the overthrow of the Somoza regime as a matter of national security explains the tenacity of Castro's own involvement in organizing, advising, and coordinating plans along these lines, beginning with the appointment of his personal envoy and ambassador to Nicaragua, Pino Machado. Soviet interests also focused on Central America, and Nicaragua in particular, although they centered more on geopolitical considerations and Nicaragua's strategic location. Because Somoza was a staunch U.S. ally, and because the possibility existed under Somoza that the United States might find it expedient to resume plans to build a canal across the isthmus in the event that the Panama Canal became inaccessible, its denial would strengthen Soviet-Cuban aims, geopolitically and otherwise.[13] In sum, Somoza's overthrow would not only serve to resolve Castro's national security concerns while strengthening Cuba's role as a strategic ally of the Soviet Union in Central America, but also block U.S. efforts to build a canal through Nicaragua.

Yet real inroads on this front did not become possible until after the Cuban missile crisis of 1962, when assurances were made that the United States would not invade Cuba if the Soviet Union removed all offensive nuclear missiles from the Cuban mainland. In perspective, it seems difficult to understand how the United States could have agreed to this arrangement in exchange for the Soviet withdrawal of offensive missiles, unless the Soviets also agreed to Cuba's demilitarization. Even Washington's non-aggression pledge was in conflict with the administration's own statements at the time, including the Joint Resolution of Congress of October 3, 1962, recommending that the United States take "whatever means may be necessary, including the use of arms, to prevent the Marxist-Leninist regime in Cuba from extending its aggression or subversive activities to any part of the hemisphere."[14] Under these circumstances, therefore, it was axiomatic that only Cuba's demilitarization could have ensured that outcome.

Thus the Soviet initiative of placing its offensive missiles in Cuba ultimately came to serve its true purposes, even though the missiles themselves were allegedly removed, and even though the Kennedy administration perceived the outcome to have been one of defeat for this unprecedented initiative. In fact, one of Khrushchev's main problems after October 1962 was not the issue of defeat, but the issue of mounting the next initiative so that Soviet interests in Cuba would not be threatened thereby nor diminished. That this task should have fallen to Khrushchev's successor might have been expected, since regrouping after Khrushchev's fall in 1964 followed without incident.

By 1965, then, there was every indication that the Moscow Conference of 1960 would be repeated on an even larger scale, with the convening of the Tricontinental Conference of African,

Asian, and Latin American Communist parties in January 1966. Numbering eighty-three radical Third World groups, the meeting of some 600 delegates in Havana was described by Spruille Braden, a former U.S. ambassador to Cuba, as "the largest gathering of guerrillas in history." Although there were few news stories on the conference to appear in the U.S. press, a former Foreign Service officer who covered the conference wrote that Moscow's hand as its "chief planner" was unmistakable.[15] More openly than ever before, the USSR had taken the initiative in juggling its strategies in support of wars of national liberation and in its sponsorship of state terrorism, the latter being a Siamese twin of the former. Under Moscow's new leadership then, all pretense of nonintervention in the affairs of other nations was discarded, as the delegates openly committed themselves to the principle of violence in overthrowing governments not meeting their approval. Havana was selected as the future headquarters for the intensification of coordinated guerrilla operations in Latin America and beyond. Though the example of Castro's contribution to liberation warfare had previously been acknowledged by Khrushchev, by 1966 Castro's tactics were seen as a model to be followed. Even Andrei A. Gromyko, Soviet foreign minister, obliquely paid tribute to Castro's achievement on the eve of the Havana meeting, stating that the Soviet Union would do everything possible to help consolidate the struggle against imperialist aggression. And on January 2, 1966, in a message primed to set the tone of the conference, both Leonid Brezhnev and Aleksei Kosygin stated in part: "Today, Havana attracts the attention of all fighters against the forces of imperialist aggression and colonialism, and for the national and social liberation of peoples. . . ."[16] Thereafter, important gains were announced at the conclusion of the Tricontinental Conference. Cuba obtained recognition for the first continental group to emerge from the conference, with the creation of the Latin American Solidarity Organization (OLAS) on January 19. An important Soviet aim was also achieved. This was to give major support to guerrilla leaders, rather than to the established Communist parties in appreciation of the tactics employed by Castro in his bid for power in Cuba in 1957 and 1958.[17] Lastly, it was the optimism behind Moscow's support for armed violence in 1966, an optimism that would not easily be defeated, that ought to be a warning to policymakers today, much as it should have been a warning to policymakers preoccupied with Southeast Asia at the time as to Soviet ambitions in Latin America. The two fronts in Latin America then being prepared—led by Che Guevara in Bolivia and by the Sandinistas in Nicaragua—would later mirror in action the radical aspirations of those then departing Havana and the Tricontinental Conference in January 1966.

The Sandinistas, it should be remembered, had launched their campaign in the jungles and mountains along the Honduran border in August 1967. Their main offensive began at a place called Pancasán, a mountain peak east of Matagalpa, where they encountered Nicaragua's National Guard. In short, the FSLN was destroyed as an active guerrilla force, including the loss of its main leaders. Those who survived—Tomás Borge and Carlos Fonseca, among others—took refuge in Cuba, where the Sandinista Front would again be reborn.[18] Guevara's armed struggle also came to an end in the jungles of Bolivia. The difference between the two fronts lay in the fact that, unlike Bolivia, Nicaragua remained a security threat to Castro's Cuba and Moscow's future Caribbean satellite.

The New Marxist-Leninist Alignment

But for two reasons, the collapse of the Sandinista insurgency in northern Nicaragua in 1967 would have led to its demise. One reason owed to the determination of Fidel Castro, and in some measure to his Soviet overseers. A second reason owed to the mind-set of Pancasán's survivors and their belief that the name of Augusto Sandino would aid their cause in overthrowing the Somoza regime. Like Castro before them, who invoked the name of José Marti as his inspiration and cause, the Sandinistas believed that using Sandino's name would invoke a liberal past, at once nationalist and mystical; that is, though Sandino was not anti–United States—only anti-interventionist—the Sandinistas opted to exploit both: being nationalist and being against Somoza meant being Sandinist and anti-Yankee. It did not matter to the Sandinistas that General Sandino was only against interventionism, or that his sole purpose was to restore Nicaragua's sovereignty; what mattered was that Sandino should provide a "mask" for their planned revolution once Somoza was removed from power.[19]

The problem for the Sandinistas, as for Castro and his overseers, was how to reach that goal. In the interval, the Soviets had other plans for their Cuban client, and Castro's own plans did not always coincide. Yet in any showdown over power, Castro remained at the mercy of his overlords. In short, Cuba's pending subjugation in foreign affairs, as in domestic affairs, would have important implications for that country's future, for its people, for its regional neighbors, and for the future of U.S. policy in the region. Indeed, the realignment of Cuba's foreign policy, beginning in 1969, would come to mean more than toeing the Soviet line. A former DGI defector, Orlando Castro Hidalgo, tells of his frustration in seeing the influx of Moscow's elite and of Cuba being made to serve the economic and foreign policy interests of the Kremlin, not of Cuba's people and their revolution. Thus control over Cuba's foreign policy was to be solidified through Moscow's control over Cuba's DGI. In the words of Castro Hidalgo, Cuba was now "a Soviet tool." Only where fundamental "Soviet diplomatic and commercial interests are not involved," he added, would Cuba "be permitted to undertake revolutionary adventures."[20] Far reaching, then, was the secret treaty signed between Cuba and the Soviets in 1969. Under its provisions whereby Cuba would lose control over its foreign policy in return for stepped-up Soviet aid, Moscow agreed to provide 5,000 technicians to be distributed among Cuba's armed forces, mining, fishing, and agricultural sectors, not to mention Cuba's intelligence services, the DGI in particular. In turn, the Soviets would increase their shipments of raw materials and agricultural machinery and their volume of purchases from Cuba. Moscow would also re-equip Castro's armed forces with advanced weapons, including surface-to-air missiles.[21] For his part, Castro agreed to desist from making any anti-Soviet public statements and to accept the historic role that the Communist parties play, especially in Latin America.

Overall, the Soviet-Cuban secret accord envisaged a double strategy. One was that the new alignment would provide the Soviet Union with a secure base for expanding its economic and geopolitical interests in the region. The second was that it opened the way, successfully as it turned out, for exporting revolution onto the Central American isthmus.[22] For Castro, the agreement served to help reconstitute the Sandinista front, since the reorganization of Cuba's Liberation Directorate flowed from that agreement. The old LN was abolished and a new Directorate (DLN) was created, with Manuel Piñeiro Losada reappointed to head it after relinquishing his post as head of the DGI.[23] Still, a problem remained that would persist for the reconstituted Liberation Directorate until 1974: the lack of a direct subsidy. Consequently, for the next five years the small sector of the Cuban economy not directly subsidized by Moscow would provide a modicum of support for the new Sandinista cadres. Yet it was during these lean years that the Sandinistas widely publicized a statement of their goals and gained new recruits. The FSLN's statement of 1969 was not unlike that of Castro's own years before, in 1953. It, too, called for the confiscation of capitalist and agricultural holdings in Nicaragua, and compensation only for those who supported their program against Somoza. The nationalization of Somoza's properties was given special emphasis, as was the FSLN's statement in its anti-Yankee aspects. Thus the latter called for the abolition of the Bryan-Chamorro Treaty (1916), which gave the United States exclusive rights to construct an interoceanic canal in Nicaragua. The document also reflected the fundamental mission of the FSLN, in that it called for the support of other liberation movements throughout the region, with the express purpose of liberating Central America from what the FSLN referred to as Yankee imperialism.[24]

As to the new recruits, they entered the ranks of the FSLN after being trained in the Soviet bloc or in Moscow. Henry Ruiz, for example, a future Sandinista leader, would receive his political education at Patrice Lumumba University (a KGB institution), as would Leticia Herrera, who joined the FSLN in 1970. Later, after the revolution, it was Herrera who also became a national leader as head of the infamous Sandinista Defense Committees, in Nicaragua.[25] Accordingly, between 1974 and 1979, the Sandinistas would mount a concerted effort by force and subversion to overthrow the Somoza regime, though differences over strategy and tactics dogged the Sandinistas in pursuit of that common goal until 1977. Such FSLN differences have been told elsewhere, perhaps by none better than ex-Sandinista Humberto Belli. As Belli explains, one key was to establish a front that included the main representative groups in Nicaraguan society opposed to Somoza. Initiated in 1977 by the Ortega brothers, two of Nicaragua's Castroite leaders, it was just such a strategy that took shape with the creation by the FSLN of the group known as "the Twelve." The other was to unify the various Sandinista factions, and this was achieved by Castro himself, preceded by secret trips to facilitate this purpose by Castro's later ambassador to Jamaica and South Yemen, Armando Ulises Estrada.[26] Unification was essential, as Castro knew, since the Soviets would only finance Cuban operations where national liberation cadres combined united front tactics, the "two-stage" revolutionary strategy endorsed by Lenin and his heirs since 1917.[27]

In retrospect, the election of Salvador Allende as the head of Chile's Popular Front Unity coalition in 1970, and the collapse of his regime just three years later, seemed to confirm the correctness of the Soviet reversal on supporting joint insurgent–united front tactics instead of emphasizing the united front and subordinating the military to the political struggle. Again, the weakness of the latter, as demonstrated in the case of Guatemala, became all too apparent in the next few years. Allende, in failing to neutralize more rapidly the anti-Communist resistance within the economic infrastructure, and especially within Chile's police and armed forces, made his regime vulnerable to these same opposition forces.[28] Accordingly, it must have been the decisive lesson for power worshippers like Brezhnev to abandon further attempts to emphasize the peaceful road to socialism in Latin America, and to readopt Castro's strategy, emphasizing armed struggle and subversion.

Indeed, the failure of the Chilean experiment in socialism strengthened anew Castro's hand and restored his influence on the stage of Soviet world strategy. Making the most of it, he lost no time in reorganizing Cuba's DLN. His new, expanded Liberation Directorate became the America Department (Departamento América), or DA, appointing once more his confidant Manuel Piñeiro to head it in 1974.[29] Castro also made sure that the DA would qualify for direct Soviet support. Earlier, he had been assured of Moscow's backing in working against countries like Nicaragua, when the Soviets permitted him to reassign Piñeiro from the DGI to head the Liberation Directorate. It is noteworthy, too, that Castro's renewed efforts in focusing on Central America, and Nicaragua in particular, would be rewarded by his Soviet counterparts, as Moscow dramatically increased economic assistance to Cuba between 1974 and 1976, from $338 million to $1,569 million, the largest increase in Soviet aid to Cuba for any two-year period since 1959.[30]

Yet the Soviet-Cuban accord of 1969 also enhanced the KGB's control over covert operations from Cuba and throughout the region. Equally important in that connection was the appointment of Yuri Andropov, just two years before, as head of the KGB. When he succeeded Brezhnev in 1982, Andropov became the first KGB chief to be appointed party secretary, but his own death came only fifteen months after taking office.

Western observers need to be reminded of Andropov's influence since the late 1960s: He came to the KGB from his post as supervisor of the Soviet empire, went on to restore the KGB's power in foreign operations "two or three times over," raised the blackness of state terrorism to new heights, and avowed, as of April

1982, that "the future belongs to socialism." In sum, the KGB under Andropov remained not "merely an instrument of the party but, to a certain extent, an interpreter of the party's will."[31] Certainly these are implications enough to warrant closer analysis of Andropov, and his years in power at the head of the KGB from 1967 to 1982, in contrast to his image in the Western media at the time as a closet liberal.[32]

The year 1969 also marked the onset of Moscow's policy of détente toward the West. The new policy accorded with perceived economic and political requirements, as well as with Moscow's tactical retreat in de-emphasizing support of national liberation movements between 1969 and 1974. It was to be the beginning of a pattern in Soviet foreign policy, although that tendency was not apparent at the time. Before 1969, for example, Soviet economic ties with the West had been minimal. Even Soviet credits with the West were few. But within five years all this began to change, with Western credits to the USSR amounting to some $13 billion, and by 1978, $50 billion. British bank loans to Moscow were largest, followed by France, Germany, and the United States. That the Soviets had approached the West for such credits almost out of desperation, and that real food shortages had to be averted, seems almost to have been forgotten. Nonetheless, the loans actually permitted the Soviets to strengthen their continued military buildup, even as the practical abandonment of the embargo on the sale of strategic materials allowed Moscow to purchase "the miniature ball bearings absolutely necessary for the construction of guidance systems" for their long-range nuclear missiles and multiple nuclear warheads.[33]

Détente, then, provided a "breathing spell" for the Soviet leaders. Otherwise, détente accorded, as did the policy of peaceful coexistence, with the Leninist policy of pursuing war by other means. In truth, détente went further than Khrushchev's coexistence policy by accelerating it. That this shift took place, and that it would be accelerated after 1974, during the next phase of détente, will be shown in the following chapter. Yet even before 1974, no clearer indication of that trend can be found than in Brezhnev's early clarification of that policy, when he stated that détente "in no way implies the possibility of relaxing the ideological struggle. On the contrary, we must be prepared for this struggle to be intensified and becoming an *even sharper form of confrontation between the two systems.*"[34] In 1976 and 1977, its intent was even codified by its inclusion in Soviet and Cuban law. Thus Article 28 of the revised Soviet constitution avowed that Soviet foreign policy aimed at the consolidation of world socialism by "supporting the struggle of peoples for national liberation and . . . preventing wars of aggression. . . ."[35] Similarly, Article 12 of the final draft of Cuba's constitution avowed as its aim to recognize "the legitimacy of wars of national liberation," even obliging Cuba to help those peoples struggling "for their liberation" as "its internationalist right and duty."[36]

Moscow's détente policy thus strengthened its tricontinental policy in supporting national liberation wars in Africa, Asia, and Latin America. The Soviet leaders never sought to address the open contradiction, even with international law, between their two contending policies: détente with the West and revolutionary action in supporting Cuba against its neighbors. By 1977, it was even beginning to appear that Moscow intended to "link" the destiny of the Soviet Union itself with that of the Third World, or so it appeared to some at the time. In any event, Moscow's policy of détente disguised its real purposes of being indistinguishable from the practice of realpolitik, a policy it condemned its Western adversaries for practicing.[37]

Clearly, where Central America is concerned, with Cuba as Moscow's client state, the aim of exporting revolution to Nicaragua and throughout Central America and the Caribbean constituted an act of war, requiring the right of self-defense under Article 51 of the United Nations Charter. That this did not happen is one of the tragedies of our time, since the United States failed to take appropriate legal and other action under Article 51, and under its own regional agreements under Article 51, to prevent the violent overthrow of Nicaragua's government in 1979.[38] As time passes, and with the hindsight of later study and reflection, one can only assume that this will also be the verdict of future historians of American foreign policy.

2

From Revolution
to Leninist State

INTERVENTION, REVOLUTION,
AND FOREIGN POLICY

In 1977, ten years after the Sandinista Front collapsed in northern
Nicaragua, the FSLN again appeared to be on the verge of collapse.
Carlos Fonseca had died the year before, the movement's helms-
man and chief ideologist. Moreover, Nicaragua appeared to have
contained the Sandinistas and to be closer to replacing the Somoza
regime with an appealing opposition leader in the person of Pedro
Joaquín Chamorro, publisher of *La Prensa*, and titular head of the
Democratic Union of Liberation (UDEL). Politically, then, the
future seemed destined "to belong, not to the revolutionaries, but
to the democratic opposition" gathering around Chamorro and the
UDEL.[1] Economically, also, Nicaragua was recovering from the
1972 earthquake that had destroyed some 600 square blocks of
downtown Managua, as relief supplies were provided to the dev-
astated area by the United States and other countries. Indeed, by
the 1970s, Nicaragua had the highest standard of living per capita
of any Central American country. In short, Nicaragua's electrifi-

cation, hydroelectric dams, hard-surfaced highways, and a climate to attract foreign investment were all much in evidence.[2] It would seem that only the credulous could believe the Soviet version of Nicaragua's popular uprising against Somoza—namely, that it was brought about by the "unbearable living conditions" of Nicaraguans under the old regime. Moscow's leader also denounced as untrue the claim that the Soviets or Cubans had anything to do with Nicaragua's revolution, since its ultimate cause, according to Mikhail Gorbachev, was to be found in the United States' imperialist exploitation of Central America.[3]

In truth, though, only a planned and organized effort can account for the next twenty-four months of descent into political and social chaos. Unfortunately, in view of that impending descent, it is instructive to note the leftward shift in the Carter administration's foreign policy toward Latin America during 1977–1980, and that Carter's own commitment to human rights actually played into the hands of the Sandinistas and their Cuban masters. Suffice to add that the two Panama Canal treaties, followed by the quasi-opening of diplomatic relations with Cuba in 1978, with the establishment of an "interest section" through the Czech Embassy in Washington, was the encouragement Castro needed to accelerate his plan of subversion against Somoza. Fueled anew by Soviet support for wars of national liberation, the Cuban-backed FSLN advanced its strategy against Nicaragua, as the Soviets continued to advance theirs through the KGB-controlled Cuban DGI while still supporting the outlawed Nicaraguan Socialist party.[4] In essence, it was the same strategy that had brought Castro to power in 1959, when the Soviets supported not one but two Communist parties. Likewise, the extent of Castro's involvement in overthrowing Somoza can be gauged from his successful effort in isolating Somoza from Nicaragua's neighbors, through his respective overtures to Panama in 1977 and Mexico in 1979.

Yet even these elaborate plans may have failed had it not been for the assassination of Pedro Joaquín Chamorro in January 1978. Thus the tragedy of Chamorro's death on January 10, compounded by the failure of the Carter administration to provide new military aid to the Somoza regime, further played into the hands of the Sandinistas. Not unexpectedly, Chamorro's assassination (he had opposed the Sandinistas) prompted an immediate meeting of FSLN leaders in Costa Rica, according to Nicaraguan military intelligence. Indeed, the agenda of that meeting was to decide how best to take advantage of Chamorro's fateful end. As a terrorist front, the Sandinistas' strategy seemed obvious: to promote civil unrest and blame the assassination on the Somoza regime. According to Jeffrey St. John, of Mutual Radio, in Managua at the time, there were in reality two assassinations carried out in Managua in January 1978: the murder of one of Latin America's most prominent editors and "the character assassination of the President of Nicaragua." St. John added only that one does not "know which assassination deserves more condemnation."[5] Hence, in the aftermath of that event the initiative passed to the Sandinistas, as the opportunity for action likewise passed to Cuba's Fidel Castro.

Accordingly, via the Soviet bloc, Cuba began transporting large-scale weapons shipments through Panama to the Sandinista command post in Costa Rica. Castro also provided close support through the training of some 300 Sandinistas in Cuba, in preparation for the guerrilla insurgency to come. Similarly, DA personnel in Costa Rica, the focal point of Cuba's support base, would also come to occupy important positions in Nicaragua once the Sandinistas succeeded in overthrowing Somoza. DA's Julián Díaz would become Cuba's first ambassador to Nicaragua since Pino Machado, while another DA official, Andrés Barahona, redocumented as a Nicaraguan, would come to serve as an upper-echelon official in the Sandinistas' future intelligence service.[6]

The sense that the Carter administration had abdicated control over events by trying to shape the outcome in Nicaragua can be seen through the testimony of witnesses at the time. General Gordon Sumner, for example, as chairman of the Inter-American Defense Board (IADB) from 1975 to 1978, testified that it was apparent in November 1977 that the United States should not vote to approve the Canal treaties, since General Omar Torrijos could no longer be trusted to support policies conducive to stability in the region. In consequence, General Sumner so notified the Chairman of the Joint Chiefs, General George Brown. Torrijos had made it clear that he would support the Sandinistas, and even planned to use Air Panama to smuggle arms to the FSLN. That the United States would permit a plan to go forward which would polarize the region—between Left and Right, between the so-called good guys on the left and bad guys on the right—not to mention illegally supplying arms to the former, made "a mockery" of President Carter's human-rights policy in the hemisphere, the former chairman of the IADB concluded.[7]

Aware of that shift, which was even common knowledge among members of the Organization of American States, Mexico fell in line with Torrijos. Thus, in retrospect, Castro's Mexican overture for aid to the Sandinistas looked easy, as Mexico's new foreign secretary, Jorge Castañeda, hastily presided over a meeting between President López Portillo and Fidel Castro on the Mexican island of Cozumel on May 16, 1979. The meeting itself was unprecedented, since it was the first time a Mexican president had met with Castro since the latter's rise to power in Cuba in 1959. In fact, before the meeting adjourned, each agreed "to establish closer bilateral relations and work for a new international economic order."[8] Alas, just three days later, Mexico's López Portillo would take another step by severing diplomatic relations with President Somoza's government. It, too, was unprecedented, since Portillo's action violated the "Estrada Doctrine," a rule by tradition in Mexican foreign relations which held that the authority of another state should not be compromised, regardless of its ideology or politics. Mexico's about-face thus opened the door to needed aid in the form of oil, liberal credit terms, advisers, technicians, and large sums of money to the Sandinistas.[9]

Mexico's decision to aid the FSLN all but sealed the fate of Nicaragua's government and the future of democracy in that besieged country. Ultimately, though, the outcome in Nicaragua rested on U.S. foreign policy under President Carter, since U.S. policy, by virtue of U.S. power, remained the final arbiter. In short, the United States intervened by abdicating its responsibilities. A last, if futile, effort was made by the then Nicaraguan Vice President Luis Pallais, who tried to convey that sense of responsibility in testimony before a House subcommittee in June 1979. Pallais reminded his U.S. audience that if Nicaragua fell to the Sandinistas, that the United States would "rue the day it lacked the resolve to contain this expansion of Soviet imperialism on this continent."[10]

The stand on the Sandinistas that Nicaragua's vice president had taken before Congress in 1979 was based on solid evidence. Unlike Castro before he came to power, the FSLN had not hidden its identity. The Sandinista program of seizing power by force would follow Castro's lead, even though many Nicaraguans—and there were many—overlooked the FSLN's platform of May 1977, the *General Political-Military Platform of the FSLN for the Triumph of the Popular Sandinista Revolution*. That document differed from previous statements only in stating the FSLN's ideology with greater clarity. The lengthy statement was unremitting in its criticism of so-called bourgeois democracy, and noted that the FSLN represented a radically different course marked out for them by Marx, Engels, Lenin, and Sandino.[11] In brief, the notion that the Sandinistas offered a "democratic alternative" was little more than a hoax. Nonetheless, as their chances of seizing power improved, they turned democratic for tactical and pragmatic reasons, agreeing to principles of political pluralism, a mixed economy, and a nonaligned foreign policy. Yet not more than two months after taking power, in July 1979, the leadership called a secret meeting of the FSLN's cadres to assess the current situation and to lay plans for consolidating the Sandinista regime in perpetuity. The "72-Hour Document" of September 1979 thus provides a blueprint of early Sandinista strategy and policy, and of the perception of the FSLN's key role within the Soviet-Cuban imperial system.[12]

The "72-Hour Document" did not surface publicly until 1985, and it was not discussed in any English-language publication until that time. Why this occurred is not entirely clear.[13] Yet the document underscored the Marxist-Leninist program and ideology of the Sandinistas, and of the FSLN as the "vanguard party" in leading the class struggle, not just in Nicaragua but throughout the region. It thus revealed their intentions of supporting wars of national liberation and of taking a leading role in the support of state terrorism. These facts, and the revelation that the "72-Hour Document" had been sent to Washington in December 1979 by Ambassador Lawrence Pezzullo, makes it all the more puzzling why the Carter administration went along with the FSLN's policy of deception by continuing to provide the Sandinista regime with sizable amounts of aid.[14] It was entirely understandable, then, when the House Committee on Intelligence finally acted to halt continued financial support to the Sandinistas. According to Herbert Romerstein, the House Intelligence Committee called a secret meeting of the House of Representatives to consider information that the committee wanted presented concerning Sandinista terrorism. It was only the third time in nearly 200 years that the House of Representatives had held such a secret session. The historic session met on February 25, 1980. As Romerstein relates, the House voted 392 to 3 to compel the president, before granting any further aid, to certify that the Sandinista regime "had not cooperated" in acts of terrorism. President Carter signed that certification on September 12, 1980,[15] at a time when the first Soviet bloc military aid and supplies to the Sandinistas would total more than 1,000 metric tons.[16]

Sandinista strategy thus represented a policy of aggression even while the United States was providing every possible assistance, and when counterrevolutionary forces inside Nicaragua were still virtually nonexistent. Equally instructive was the character of Soviet-Cuban involvement in aiding sub rosa the FSLN, though hardly with aid of a constructive kind. Miguel Bolaños Hunter, for example, who worked for Nicaragua's State Security Department (DGSE), attested to the close support provided by the Soviet government within days of the FSLN's takeover in Nicaragua. He explained that five Soviet generals and vice-generals had come to advise Sandinista Chief of Staff Joaquín Cuadra as early as August 1979, and that the Soviets, even then, "made all of the crucial decisions on weapons and aid."[17] Also instructive was the incre-

mental nature of Soviet diplomatic involvement, since th
Union maintained no formal diplomatic presence in th
before the mid–1970s. Hence, only two days after the Sa
reached power, on July 21, 1979, the Soviets intimated a desire to
normalize diplomatic relations with Nicaragua. By mid–October,
this was an accomplished fact, though the first Soviet Embassy
personnel did not begin arriving in Managua until January 1980.[18]
Extensive agreements followed, like those signed with Grenada
before mid–1983. Thereupon, talks with Kremlin leaders on a wide
range of subjects began in March 1980, when Sandinista ministers
of interior, planning, and defense first visited the Soviet capital.
Documents signed included an agreement on establishing party-
to-party relations, an agreement on cultural and scientific cooperation, a consular convention, and a trade agreement. Others
included an economic and technical cooperation agreement, and
an air-traffic accord. Under the latter with Aeroflot, two flights a
week between Moscow and Managua via Havana were scheduled
to begin operations. And both countries agreed to cooperate in
developing Nicaragua's mining industry, in addition to transport
and communication. Lastly, under Moscow's initial military
agreement with Nicaragua, the Soviets would provide some $125
million between 1980 and 1982, including 250 Soviet technical
and military personnel and a range of armaments comprising fifty
T-54/55 tanks, missiles, transport aircraft, and anti-aircraft guns.[19]
Indeed, on December 21, 1982, Yuri Andropov, as Brezhnev's
successor and as head of the Soviet Defense Council, vowed
Moscow's support for worldwide "liberation" in order to facilitate
the advance of the peoples of Asia, Africa, the Arab East, and Latin
America.[20]

The only greater involvement in Nicaragua's so-called popular
revolution was the extent of Cuban intervention. According to
Miguel Bolaños Hunter's testimony, Cubans were the most visible
among Soviet bloc advisers in State Security, Nicaragua's equivalent of Cuba's DGI, and in the Department of Propaganda and
Political Education.[21] In fact, the Sandinista triumph had been a
personal one for Castro's foreign policy after more than twenty

years of isolation in the Caribbean. Thus Cuba experts were not left to wonder when Castro flew to Nicaragua in July 1980, on the eve of the FSLN's celebratory activities, to mark the occasion of the Sandinistas' first year in power. There, Castro even held a secret meeting in Monimbó to underscore his part in overthrowing Somoza's government. At this meeting, according to credible intelligence sources, were Cuban agents on leave from their posts in the United States; the head of Cuba's DA, Manuel Piñeiro Losada; Dudley Thompson, then Minister of National Security in the Jamaican government; René Theodor, secretary-general of Cuba's Communist party, and other revolutionaries from Guatemala, El Salvador, and Mexico. According to these same intelligence sources, Castro is said to have boasted that he had the capacity to inflict great harm on the United States through terrorist action, and that the *yanquis* cannot begin to imagine Cuba's terrorist capabilities. Noting the riots that had occurred in Miami during the spring of 1980, he added that Cuba could accomplish things that would make the riots in Florida "look like a sunshower."[22]

The Social Order Transformed

In the remainder of this chapter, the consequences of the Soviet-Cuban assault on Nicaragua are examined through an analysis of the FSLN's Ministry of Interior (MINT). In brief, MINT had only two functions from the beginning: to exercise complete political control over the country through outside assistance and to ensure the regime's survival as the dominant political force inside Central America. The violence of attempting to control the conduct of Nicaragua's peoples is also considered, since such a purpose goes to the root of the problem of Marxism-Leninism as an ideology and as a political phenomenon.

MINT, of course, is Nicaragua's equivalent of Castro's Ministry of Interior (MININT) in Cuba. At its head is Tomás Borge, the only surviving member of the original Sandinista leaders and one of the FSLN's nine *comandantes* on the ruling Sandinista Directorate. The interior ministry could not have begun to enlarge itself and thereby widen its activities without the help of the Soviet Union, the Soviet bloc, and Cuba's buildup of State Security (DGSE), a department of MINT. So extensive did MINT operations become that it very soon comprised 3 directorates-general, 13 directorates, 43 departments, and more than 15,000 people. The DGSE, for example, which is regulated by the KGB-controlled Cuban DGI, alone employs some 3,000 people under Lenin Cerna, DGSE's chief.[23]

MINT's control extends to the nation's telephone and postal systems, communications, security, and penal systems. MINT also produces propaganda, censors the media, and publishes the Sandinista party newspaper, *Barricada*. MINT likewise controls the flow of information to senior officials through its daily intelligence summaries, provides military intelligence, and even controls the *turbas divinas*, the Sandinista mobs used to intimidate dissenters and crush virtually all political opposition. Indeed, the severity of Borge's Interior Ministry in controlling opposition has been massively documented with reference to public opinion, religious groups, and the independent press. Even public sentiment is monitored through one of MINT's departments, created for this purpose: the Ideological Diversionism Department.[24] Most important, however, for controlling and suppressing political parties and dissent is the DSGE. Alvaro José Baldizón Avilés, formerly Chief Investigator of Special Operations, has testified as to the wide-ranging illegal activities of MINT, from political assassinations to drug trafficking for money in order to support clandestine operations by State Security outside Nicaragua. Baldizón testified, for example, that a MINT directive issued in 1982 required that all cocaine, precious metals, and U.S. dollars received during MINT operations be rendered to MINT in order to support its international operations[25]—that is, to support Sandinista-sponsored terrorism, particularly for guerrilla operations directed against such neighboring states as El Salvador.

MINT's reach is thus uncontrolled inside Nicaragua. Indeed, the first decisive step taken to ensure that outcome was in August

1981, when the last independent poll was conducted. It revealed that after two years of Sandinista rule, only 28 percent of Nicaragua's people supported the new government and 60 percent opposed it. In reaction, the Sandinista Directorate issued Decree 888, banning the taking of any further independent polls and surveys.[26] So concerned was MINT, because of the pending national election of November 1984, that the DGSE was ordered to conduct ad hoc opinion polls to measure the extent of the political opposition's popularity. These ad hoc polls were conducted for one main reason: to allow the Sandinistas to develop a strategy so as to neutralize the opposition vote in that election. According to Baldizón, the intensification of MINT's efforts to manipulate the election's outcome can be gauged from the fact that two new departments were created to collect and assess "street conversation" on the eve of the 1984 election, to deal with potential trouble spots, and to assess polling results. Consequently, in 1984, the DGSE formed the Department for Control of the Social Foundation to coordinate its efforts with the Anti-Counterrevolutionary Department; the latter monitored supporters of the democratic opposition, making arrests when necessary, while the Territorial Department, working with the Sandinista Defense Committees, monitored counterrevolutionary activities countrywide.[27]

In its severity, then, the consequences of Sandinista rule represented what can only be described as a series of traumatic shocks to Nicaraguan society. The first shock was the revolution itself, measured against what the democratic opposition expected in place of a Somoza-type regime. The second shock was caused by such governmental institutions as MINT: the Sandinista mobs and their destructive use, the Defense Committees (CDSs) and their involvement in repression, the open persecution of the Catholic Church, the terror inflicted against Nicaragua's indigenous peoples, the militarization of society, and the countless political arrests of FSLN opponents generally.[28] A third shock involved the "liquidation" of illiteracy, a cruel hoax. The real objective of the regime's literacy campaign was not to educate but to imbue students with the aims and purposes of the Sandinistas' ideology and FSLN revolutionary goals. In violation of the American Convention on Human Rights, which the Sandinista government ratified in November 1979, the new government subsequently ignored the recognition of the "preferential rights" of parents to choose the type of education they desire for their children, which was guaranteed under that Convention.[29] In summary, students, teachers, and parents were subjected to MINT's guidelines of what could be taught in Nicaragua's educational institutions. Thus elementary school textbooks instructed students to add by counting grenades and bullets; they were taught to hate the United States,[30] and they were instructed instead to be followers of Carlos Fonseca, founder of the FSLN.[31]

As in the case of the Soviet Union and also Cuba, Nicaraguan society and its way of life are being incrementally destroyed by a process aptly described as the "infantilization" of the individual.[32] And that process, as others have testified, leads to increased collectivization, to the destruction of freedom, and to the moral, psychological, and social impairment of the individual and of the society.

3

The Sandinistas
and Human Rights

FSLN'S INTERNAL WAR

Before the Sandinistas seized power on July 19, 1979, they accepted the resolution of the Organization of American States to support a democratic regime in Nicaragua; they agreed to OAS conditions to hold free elections "within a few weeks," to respect human rights and civil liberties, and to follow a nonaligned foreign policy.[1] Yet, as the previous chapter evidenced, the whole of the FSLN's commitment to democratic principles was one vast deception. General Omar Torrijos, who characterized the Sandinistas as "good old boys," had engaged in what can only be described as myth making. He, too, had been a victim of deception.[2]

Significantly, the FSLN was not inclined to reveal its intentions at the outset of Nicaragua's popular revolution against Somoza in July 1979. So advised by Castro, they knew that their plans and purposes would not be supported by the Nicaraguan people. And, indeed, it was human rights violations that would become the source of much disillusionment on the part of those who eventually defected. As one disillusioned defector later acknowledged, "the Nicaraguan Marxist-Leninist regime, as well as any other type of

Marxist-Leninist regime throughout the world, can only stay in power through massive repression against the people." The same Soviet-trained ex-official held that most economic failures can be attributed to the false premise that underlies the Marxist-Leninist approach to human welfare; noting that the FSLN operates "on the mistaken assumption that labor creates the wealth of a society," he added that it is the freedom to compete, to apply human ingenuity to the solution of problems, that generates wealth.[3]

That the Sandinistas, then, would mask their real intentions was axiomatic, even though Castro also advised them to consolidate their power quickly. Hence a key element in establishing such control remained unchanged: the formation of State Security (DGSE), the apparatus to ensure that outcome, and the most important instrument for controlling opposition political groups and dissent, and the arbiter, ultimately, of human rights throughout Nicaragua.

Theoretically, MINT oversees Nicaragua's prison system, as noted in the previous chapter, although its jails for political prisoners remain under the DGSE. Understandably, the FSLN has refused to call DGSE jails "prisons" or their inmates "prisoners." Instead, euphemisms are employed; the latter are "detainees" and the former "detention centers."[4] According to the Permanent Commission on Human Rights (CPDH), the only independent organization in Nicaragua which publishes information on human rights abuses in the country, there are nine such detention centers, corresponding to each of the regime's nine designated regions. Still, the nine represent only the most visible DGSE jails, not its other clandestine prisons and private dwellings, where prisoners are interrogated for up to four or five days.[5] Moreover, DGSE-operated facilities are aided by, if not dependent upon, supervisory Cuban personnel numbering about 400, in addition, reportedly, to some 70 Soviet advisers.[6]

"El Chipote," as it is known, is probably the most feared of State Security prisons. Located on the slope of the Loma de Tiscapa hill behind Managua's Intercontinental Hotel, political detainees are brought for interrogation to this remodeled prison—remodeled so as to intimidate or even torture its detainees. Many who are detained in El Chipote are from Nicaragua's middle class, the group most often politically active in opposition to the Sandinista regime.[7] A dramatic case in point was the jailing of the FSLN's former vice-minister of justice, Alberto Gámez Ortega, who resigned his post in November 1982 rather than abide his disillusionment with the regime's justice system. Almost immediately, Gámez went from being an administrator of Sandinista justice to another of its victims. Like so many others unused to El Chipote's barbaric conditions of confinement, where Gámez was detained for nearly three months, the former vice-minister was forced to seek medical treatment in Costa Rica for some time after his release.[8]

Similarly, the jailing of José Esteban González, founding director of the CPDH, provides another dramatic instance of official repression. Although acting as head of one of Nicaragua's human rights organizations on a European trip in early 1981 to discuss such violations, the Sandinistas again acted swiftly after his return to Nicaragua. His subsequent release from political imprisonment was only made possible by the intervention of the OAS in March 1981. Nonetheless, González was subsequently tried and sentenced *in absentia* for alleged Public Order charges by the Sandinista regime.[9]

The CPDH had been an early target of FSLN reprisals because it had sought to document the wide-ranging nature of official repression, involving not just the regime's political opponents but all human rights violations. Founded in April 1977, the CPDH's original purpose was to monitor the human rights abuses of the Somoza regime, although it soon recognized an even greater need to document FSLN abuses after 1979: against former members of the old regime, the National Guard in particular, against church leaders, against independent labor unionists, against opposition-party activists, against private-sector officials, against human rights advocates, and even against defense lawyers. In all, virtually no group was exempt from official repression, as these abuses extended to the nation's *campesinos*, Miskito Indians, and Creole population, even to the little-known Jewish population of Nicaragua.[10]

Nina Shea, who testified before the House Rules Committee in June 1987 in connection with a congressional resolution to suspend action against certain Nicaraguans and Salvadorans in the United States, characterized Sandinista attacks against some of the civilian groups as bordering on genocide. These attacks, she explained, included aerial bombardment and combined air and ground attacks against innocents, especially near the towns of Nueva Guinea, Rama, and Punta Gorda.[11] Others have similarly testified. In 1985, for example, in remarks before the annual meeting of the American Society of International Law, John Norton Moore focused on such groups, including the massive campaign waged against the Miskito Indians. Again the FSLN's campaign included attacks on villages, livestock, and crops; arrest of the Indian leadership; and disbanding of the Indians' native organization as "counterrevolutionary," adding that, of some 100,000 Indians at the beginning of these atrocities, 20,000 had fled Nicaragua and another 20,000 had been moved to "relocation camps."[12]

Declaring a state of emergency, as in 1982 and again in 1985, merely gave the regime another instrument to justify the severity of its repression, as Martin Kriele has noted. Kriele also notes the parallels between the FSLN's internal war and actions carried out by the National Socialist regime under Hitler in the 1930s. Thus the Sandinista mobs were "reminiscent" of the Storm Troopers, the SA squads attacking and threatening civilians as the authorities looked on; equally compelling, he added, was the treatment accorded the Jewish minorities both in Germany at the time and in Nicaragua half a century later.[13] In the case of Nicaragua's Jewish community of some seventy families, about 350 people, Kriele's comparison is indeed compelling. According to the American Jewish Committee's investigation, it found that the entire Jewish community of Nicaragua "had vanished," having been forced into exile by the Sandinista regime.[14]

An American, Wesley Smith, who lived in Central America for two years, and who conducted hundreds of interviews during that time, tried to convey the extent of this terror in a report released in March 1986, titled *The Sandinista Prison System: A Nation Confined.* The report confirms the testimony of the many victims of the FSLN's internal war, including the experiences of Gámez and González. Focusing on the plight of political prisoners, the report cited the difficulty of establishing the number of such prisoners, but indicated that the number of "clandestine arrests" alone as high, and that the so-called floating prison population—those Nicaraguans arrested and rearrested and held for short periods under stressful conditions—as equally high. Hence the investigator's conclusion seems inescapable: that political detention was "designed to intimidate the entire country and to end opposition to the Sandinistas."[15]

From the perspective of the FSLN, the signing of the Guatemala Accords (Esquipulas II) in August 1987 marked such a turning point in their eight-year internal war. In signing the peace plan the Sandinistas gained time against their internal opponents while holding out the hope of establishing "democratic pluralism with full political rights for all Nicaraguans." In reality, Esquipulas II was intended to further the FSLN's consolidation of power, while effectively eliminating the only counterrevolutionary force that might still challenge its control—the politico-military democratic front, or United Nicaraguan Opposition (UNO), precariously supported by the United States under the Reagan Doctrine.[16] In substance, the FSLN's calculations and the political and military strategy behind that initiative—to eliminate the UNO and U.S. influence in Nicaraguan affairs— cannot be underestimated. Maintaining the deception of complying with Esquipulas II would help neutralize the UNO's counterrevolutionary force and thus draw this crucial phase of Nicaragua's internal war to a close. Eliminating U.S. influence required that no action be taken that could "modify the majority vote of the Congress" against sustaining aid to the UNO's counterinsurgency. Only in this way, as a secret FSLN document revealed, can "the strategic defeat of the counterrevolution" be assured. Like the Vietnam War, then, the Sandinistas envisage the outcome of their internal war as dependent on the victory of this selfsame war "in Washington."[17]

An Assault on World Order

The FSLN's internal war thus represents a two-pronged assault on world order in the Americas. The expansionist thrust of the FSLN's policies and the wide-ranging consequences of this other assault are examined in the following chapter and in Chapter 5, on Soviet aims. But the most visible consequences of that assault—the flight of refugees both north and south throughout Central America and beyond—may well represent the most far-reaching assault on world order possible.

Unlike the figures on the overall number of political prisoners in Nicaragua—which may number between 8,000 and 9,000—the numbers of refugees fleeing the FSLN's reign of oppression are enormous. Where major differences show, they arise over the meaning of these numbers, and whether the flow of refugees poses more than a minor problem for U.S. national interests. Policymakers, for example, acknowledge the link between Soviet expansionism in the Americas and the refugee problems created thereby, but they fail to see the issue as more than a "minor reason" for resisting Soviet expansionism. So focused are they on "the establishment of Soviet military bases and the maintenance of the balance of world power,"[18] that they cannot see the fleeing of innocents as in the same category. There are, however, a minority of policymakers who dissent from this view. Indeed, the evidence suggests that the policymaking majority is too focused on the issue of power projection, important as its main aspects are, and insufficiently focused on the no less visible threat of "economic stagnation and a mushrooming population" in Central America.[19]

In a major policy address before a joint session of Congress in April 1983, President Reagan drew attention to this issue in Central America. The address was reminiscent of President Truman's before a joint session in 1947, and the threat Marxism-Leninism posed to free peoples and democratic principles. Reagan admonished that if the United States stood by and did nothing, the countries of Central America could soon face the threat of Sandinista terrorism, with the result that the number of refugees would dramatically increase, threatening the entire region from Panama to Mexico with an influx of peoples.[20] Unlike 1947, what followed the president's call to protect free peoples went largely unheeded, except for a modicum of temporary support to aid the UNO's counterinsurgency, and except for the "liberation" of Grenada in October 1983, wresting it from the Soviet-Cuban axis in the Caribbean. Belatedly, Congress also acted, but only to pass a law to control illegal immigration to the United States. The law's only key sanction made it illegal for employers to knowingly hire or continue to employ aliens unauthorized to work in the United States; it thus empowered the Immigration and Naturalization Service to impose penalties on employers who hire undocumented aliens, except undocumented aliens who had resided in the United States between January 1982 and May 1987.[21]

Predictably, the refugee issue has assumed increasing importance as a social and political problem, an issue about which the nation's legislators had been forewarned. Its causes and the number of refugees since 1978–79 are a matter of record, though the issue's overall significance remains to be addressed.

The causes of refugee flight from Nicaragua since the late 1970s are reducible to seven, corresponding to the definition of "refugee" in international law. These include a well-founded fear of persecution for reasons of race, religion, nationality, or political opinion.[22] Religious persecution, for example, remains high on the list of causes, even though Cardinal Obando y Bravo staunchly opposed the previous regime in Nicaragua. Hence some twenty of Nicaragua's Catholic clergy have been expelled from the country without due process, and Cardinal Obando himself remains an enemy to the Sandinistas. FSLN attacks against civilian targets, though, stand even higher on the list of causes. Between 1984 and the end of 1986, according to recent testimony, there were thirteen military attacks reported by civilians now living in refugee camps in Costa Rica.[23] Similar attacks have been confirmed by Indian villagers assaulted by Sandinista troops along Nicaragua's Atlantic coast, with an Indians' Council of Elders reporting the destruction of forty-two villages and forty-nine churches in 1982. *Campesinos*, since they are particularly vulnerable to arbitrary arrest and detention, have been forced to seek refuge or join Nicaragua's counter-revolutionary insurgency. The remaining reasons for seeking refuge all reflect the severity of the regime's blackness: torture and ill treatment in detention, forcible resettlement, economic reprisals, and evasion of the military draft.[24]

Although the Refugee Act of 1980 closely follows the international law's definition of refugee—in that it stipulates U.S. willingness to give refugee status to peoples unable or unwilling to return to their country of origin on account of persecution or "a well-founded fear of persecution on the grounds of race, religion, nationality . . . or political opinion"—current U.S. policy has been to classify most Central Americans seeking asylum "as economic migrants and not political refugees."[25] As a result, innocents fleeing Nicaragua must invariably meet the strict legal test for political asylum, based on "a well-founded fear of persecution."

In general, the number of refugees fleeing conditions of internal war fled in three distinct waves. In the first wave—in 1978–79—when over 200,000 fled the growing signs of oppression, many sought refuge in Mexico and the United States. In the second wave—between 1980 and 1982—many were Miskito Indians and many others represented an increasing number of refugees from neighboring El Salvador and Guatemala.[26] The third wave—from 1983 to the present—mirrors a continuing flow of humanity in search of peace and the semblance of security and stability. According to the Puebla Institute in New York, a respected human rights organization, over 300,000 Nicaraguans (a number greater than 10 percent of Nicaragua's population) left the country between 1979 and 1987, with more than half that number now residing in the United States.[27] And the exodus continues at high levels, even as the Sandinistas plan for a second decade of totalitarian rule and prepare anew for regional terrorist insurgencies.

Overall, the rising impact of this continued flow of refugees from Nicaragua and from other targeted states in the region, El Salvador and Guatemala in particular, should not long delay U.S. policymakers from drawing the necessary conclusions as to the significance of this so-called minor issue in East-West relations. The influx of a larger and growing refugee population as a consequence of further Soviet-backed insurgencies in the region would inevitably pose insurmountable problems for the United States on its southern flank. Even at present levels of support, according to the General Accounting Office, the cost of resettling refugees is inordinately high. A recent study by the Office of the U.S. Coordinator for Refugee Affairs determined that, in fiscal years 1981 and 1982 alone, federal, state, and local governments spent some $3 billion to process, receive, and assist many of these refugees in the United States.[28] In summary, such data reflect an accurate accounting of the cost of human migration in the face of the Marxist-Leninist assault on world order in Central America.

In March 1986, no doubt to reemphasize the alarming significance of this issue, and three years after his address before a joint session of Congress on Central America, President Reagan again urged Congress to reconsider its importance, noting that if the counterinsurgency collapsed, the outcome would be "a vast migration march to the United States of hundreds of thousands of refugees." Indeed, by December 1988, the Immigration and Naturalization Service reported that its office in Harlingen, Texas, was receiving 2,000 applications for political asylum each week, a rate four or five times higher than six months earlier, with half coming from Nicaragua.[29]

From Consolidation
to Expanded War

THE MILITARY BUILDUP

After some thirty years, Cuba remains the key to Soviet strategic aims in the Caribbean basin, with its nearly 15,000 military, technical, and intelligence personnel stationed there. Similarly, after nearly a decade of Soviet and Soviet bloc involvement in Nicaragua, this strategic Central American state augurs to become another Cuba within the Soviet imperial system. Control over Nicaragua would extend the range of Soviet air and sea power in the region by providing seaports on both the Caribbean and Pacific coasts, a mainland base for military and intelligence networks as in Cuba, and a training and supply entrepôt for Marxist-Leninist guerrillas seeking to subvert the governments of neighboring states.[1]

Sandinista rule, in consequence, allowed for only two options upon taking power in 1979: "a revolutionary solution for the entire region given the 'ripple effect' of the Sandinista Revolution, or the eventual defeat of Nicaragua."[2] Given these options, the Sandinistas had no recourse, if they were to retain power, other than to resort to the militarization of Nicaraguan society. Above all, since the choices lay between revolution and defeat, any détente with Costa Rica and Honduras, for example, though neither state posed any military threat to the Sandinista Revolution, could only be temporary. Similarly, the notion that a détente-type relationship with the United States was possible was little more than fanciful, even as a temporary policy. Though this was not the view in Washington between 1979 and 1981, it is a measure of the distance in outlook that separated U.S. policy under Carter from the realities of post-Somoza Nicaragua under the Sandinistas. For, in fact, not only was it expedient to blame all of Somoza's wrongs on the United States, since Somoza was staunchly pro–United States, but it was also the sort of "foreign devil" view that appealed to Managua's newly installed Marxist-Leninists. Since the FSLN viewed U.S. democracy as they viewed Somoza's rule, "as a smokescreen for exploitative capitalism," there was really nothing that the United States could have done to win friends or promote détente with the new regime; and who better had helped to shape the Sandinista outlook in this regard than Castro himself? A détente-type approach, then, was not even available to the United States between 1979 and 1981, when every effort—financial and otherwise—was made to assist the new government in Managua.[3] In sum, when it is the other side that is dictating the next move— that is, the Moscow-Havana axis—the outcome may indeed lead to the defeat of U.S. interests. Were this approach allowed to play itself out in the years ahead, it would inevitably lead to the defeat of U.S. interests in a region—unlike Vietnam—that is inalienably vital to the security of the United States (see Appendix 1, Map 2).

Consequently, an immediate Sandinista priority was the need to transform their guerrilla force of some 6,000 men into a conventional army, plus a large revolutionary militia and reserve force. Yet the FSLN's plan to create the largest army in Nicaragua's history—and in Central America's—was bound to encounter formidable opposition. Once the honeymoon of the FSLN victory passed and disillusionment became widespread, voluntary enlistments declined sharply. In consequence, and out of military necessity, the FSLN adopted a variety of coercive tactics, including the use of the infamous Cuban-style "block committees" to compel Nicaraguans to enlist in the People's Army, the reserves, or the militia units.[4] When these tactics failed, the Sandinistas enacted a draft law in September 1983. Condemned by Nicaragua's Conference of Bishops as a travesty, the Bishops' pastoral letter declared the Sandinista People's Army (EPS) to be the army of a political party and not an army of the Nicaraguan state, adding that "no one can be obliged to take up arms in order . . . to benefit a political party."[5] Nonetheless, Defense Minister Humberto Ortega proclaimed the draft as mandatory, except for government workers in key jobs and those in exempt categories; otherwise, all males between the ages of 18 and 40 were eligible to be drafted. So difficult was it to enforce this law that the FSLN again resorted to coercive tactics, using "press gangs" and other methods of intimidation. When the regime sought to tighten enforcement of the draft law in late 1983, some 1,500 youths between the ages of 17 and 25 fled the country.[6]

In theory, the EPS adhered closely to Soviet military doctrine, which emphasizes the use of massed armor. Virtually starting from scratch, since the armor inherited by the regime included only three World War II tanks and twenty-five antiquated armored cars from Somoza's National Guard, the first T-55 Soviet tanks arrived in mid–1981. By 1982, the FSLN had obtained enough T-55s, the Warsaw Pact's main battle tank, to form two armored battalions; and by the beginning of 1985, enough T-55s had been delivered to permit the formation of five armored battalions of twenty-two tanks each. EPS's chief of staff, Cuban-trained Joaquín Cuadra, on being interviewed in early 1985, acknowledged the number of such tanks, adding that the Sandinistas planned to acquire a total of 150.[7] As Cuadra appeared to put a limit on the number of these tanks, it is significant that an eyewitness (a truck driver) reported counting fifty-two tanks being unloaded at Corinto not more than a month after Nicaragua signed the Guatemalan peace plan in August 1987.[8] Likewise, other weaponry began arriving as early as mid–1981 to support combat operations for long periods, even though no tangible reason existed at the time to warrant such a buildup (see Appendix 1, Map 4). Provided to bolster EPS firepower, these included Soviet-made 57-millimeter antitank guns, 122-millimeter howitzers (surpassing in range and firepower all other artillery in Central America), Soviet-made BM-21s, capable of launching a barrage of forty 122-millimeter rockets, as well as hundreds of mortars. Further support to sustain such operations arrived from the Soviet bloc and included large numbers of transport units: jeeps, flatbed trucks, tank ferries, communication vans, tanker trucks for fuel, and field kitchens.[9]

The loss of Grenada as a Soviet-Cuban asset doubtless accelerated Soviet delivery of military aid to Nicaragua, since Grenada had also been receiving large quantities of military assistance since 1981. Hence, Nicaragua's military buildup after 1983 had been assisted, in all likelihood, by the diversion of supplies that would have been earmarked for Grenada but for the U.S.-led invasion that wrested Grenada from Soviet-Cuban control in October 1983. Accordingly, in 1982 and 1983, Soviet military supplies to Nicaragua totaled 11.2 thousand tons ($140 million) and 13.9 thousand tons ($250 million), respectively, whereas in 1984 and 1985, Soviet military deliveries nearly doubled to 20 thousand tons ($370 million) and 19.4 thousand tons ($280 million), respectively.[10] By 1985, then, Sandinista cadres numbered some 30,000, with 10 regular infantry battalions, a special airborne battalion inaugurated in 1982, and special counterinsurgency battalions, while the bulk of the EPS reserves stood at 160 battalions equipped with Soviet bloc arms as the AK-47 assault rifle.[11]

The preempted decision to embrace militarism also meant building the foundation of an air force; it likewise entailed starting from scratch, since the Sandinistas inherited only a handful of AT-33A jet aircraft, transport planes, and helicopters. Accustomed to bold initiatives in the era of détente, the Soviets lost no time in initiating the first shipment of air support for the FSLN's projected 2,000-member Sandinista Air Force and Air Defense Force (FAS/DDA) with the delivery of the first two MI-8/HIP medium-lift helicopters in 1981; and in April 1982, the Soviets formally donated more MI-8s, alleging that they would be used to help develop

Nicaragua's Atlantic coastal region.[12] Instead, the MI-8s were camouflaged and armed with machine-gun and rocket pods for flying missions against Indian insurgents and against the growing ranks of a larger anti-Sandinista resistance by mid–1982.[13] To crush the growing anti-Sandinista resistance, termed "contras" by the FSLN, Moscow supplied the first MI-24/HIND D helicopters, the Soviets' principal attack helicopters then in use against Afghan rebels halfway around the world. If, moreover, delivery of the HIND D marked an unprecedented escalation of Nicaragua's military buildup, the FSLN all but crossed the Rubicon in Central America by deploying them. Indeed, first use of the HIND Ds should have provoked the most serious debate in Washington, but apparently did not.[14] The year before, in fact, FSLN's Daniel Ortega informed reporters that Nicaragua had a right to procure fighter aircraft and that the United States should not worry itself "over the brand name." No doubt his statement was prompted in part by small air raids on Managua itself in 1983, in the need to remove these embarrassing demonstrations of resistance to Sandinista rule. Thus did Ortega revive the issue again on his trip to Moscow in June 1984. Yet as MIG aircraft are of "no use for guerrilla warfare," in contrast to the HIND D, the acquisition of MIG fighters would not have fundamentally changed the already revolutionary character and buildup of the FSLN's air force.[15] In short, the HIND D added a dimension to the Sandinistas' FAS that went beyond any legitimate defensive requirements, since key targets in Honduras, Costa Rica, and El Salvador were now within reach of this flying "tank."[16]

Perhaps the most intimidating of all FAS assets, from the perspective of U.S. policymakers, has been the completion of Punta Huete, a 10,000-foot airfield—the largest in Central America—across Lake Managua from Nicaragua's capital. The airfield itself is surrounded by antiaircraft sites, as aerial photographs show, with a dispersal area and revetments to accommodate virtually any military and reconnaissance aircraft in the Soviet airfleet.[17] Although Punta Huete is currently used for sabotage training, FSLN Defense Minister Humberto Ortega has stated that the reception of MIGs is only a matter of time, while Nicaraguan pilots are trained to fly these and other aircraft in the Soviet inventory.[18]

It was unremarkable, then, when a high-level defector, Major Roger Miranda Bengoechea, surfaced in October 1987 to warn U.S. officials about the FSLN's continued and heightened military buildup. To be sure, his revelations were belatedly confirmed by Humberto Ortega, the latter revealing that some 250,000 men and women were already under arms, representing some 85,000 EPS regulars, 15,000 security police, and the remainder in militia and reserves. And the key assertion made by Miranda Bengoechea was not denied; namely, that the FSLN planned to raise the level of Nicaragua's armed forces to 600,000 by 1995, under a new defense accord with the Soviet Union.[19]

Miranda Bengoechea, who served as chief of the secretariat of Nicaragua's Ministry of Defense until his defection, disclosed aspects of this buildup at a news gathering arranged by the State Department in December 1987. Especially significant, in view of the earlier testimony of Bolaños Hunter, was Miranda's part in drafting a 68-page document in the preceding months, detailing Sandinista needs for meeting such requirements under the proposed buildup with Moscow and Soviet bloc assistance through the mid–1990s. Miranda's testimony was given added poignancy, since the Sandinistas had only signed the Guatemalan peace plan that August, which "called for limiting the size of national armies in Central America." Miranda Bengoechea also confirmed, regarding long-term planning for Nicaragua's military establishment, that these military needs were "handled by a group of senior Nicaraguan, Cuban and Soviet officials."[20] Instead of plans for peaceful and constructive purposes, as envisaged in the peace accord, the new military accord envisaged an intensified buildup to new levels of military capacity, including the shipment of 250,000 additional assault rifles, helicopters, flamethrowers, and gas masks as well as delivery of the long-delayed squadron of MIG-21 Bs.[21]

Thus has military necessity dictated FSLN policy as the means of consolidating its power. Yet this posture has been balanced by Esquipulas II to help influence international opinion, especially among liberal Democratic members of Congress distrustful of Republican policy on Central America. Yet again, though Nicaragua's arms buildup is seen as essential to consolidation, the high military outlays—between 30 and 40 percent of their annual budget—also serve as a deterrent to intervention. The defeat of the counterrevolution, finally, would free the regime to concentrate on fueling anew its expanded war, the last component of an externally supported policy seen as essential to the survival of the FSLN in power; it could then join its "strategic ally" in fueling national liberation struggles throughout Central America—and beyond.[22]

War and Political Terrorism

Terrorism, according to the architect of the Soviet system, "recognizes all methods of struggle"; indeed, as V. I. Lenin wrote, terrorism can never be rejected "in principle, nor can we ever do so."[23] Harnessed to state power for subversive ends, terrorism becomes nearly indistinguishable from clandestine war waged across national frontiers—what the Soviets euphemistically refer to as wars of national liberation.

Accordingly, it is necessary to recall Castro's America Department (DA) and its revolutionary function in the conduct of Cuba's foreign policy since 1974, when the DA took responsibility for planning the overthrow of the Somoza regime some five years later. The DA, moreover, represents an even more dangerous form of terrorism than its Middle East variety, since it avoids the sort of terrorist acts that make headlines, and that in turn might provoke some form of U.S. retaliation.[24] The analogue in Nicaragua of Castro's DA is the Department of International Relations (DRI), the department that oversees the FSLN's revolutionary policy in Central America. The counterpart of both the DA and the DRI is the USSR's International Department, the direct descendant of Lenin's Comintern and, until recently, headed by Boris Ponomarev, an ex-official of that formerly Leninist body.[25] In summary, it can be expected that the DRI will follow Cuba's DA by creating geographical sections corresponding to Central and South America, the Caribbean, and North America, and function as the FSLN's arm for planning and coordinating Nicaragua's "covert operations in support of the Cuban-Soviet . . . revolutionary strategy in Latin America."[26] Similarly, just as the DA was instrumental in targeting Nicaragua, the DRI can be expected to play a role in targeting El Salvador and Guatemala, in assisting the respective guerrilla operations in both countries, and in providing training, funding, and military assistance with Soviet bloc support. As Z. Zagladin, deputy chief of the USSR's International Department, wrote in January 1980, in linking the "victory of Nicaragua" with Soviet-Cuban strategy in the region, he hoped "that Nicaragua will 'have its continuators.'"[27]

The preceding, moreover, stands in marked contrast to the repeated claims of Nicaragua's leaders, both publicly and privately, "that their government is not involved with international terrorism" and that none of Nicaragua's "troops or arms are involved in El Salvador." Sandinista leaders have also told members of Congress "that they cannot be responsible for the acts of individual Nicaraguans who help the Salvadoran left."[28] These denials are in keeping with both DRI and DA policy, since both are expected to avoid actions that could build a consensus to punish either Cuba or Nicaragua, despite more than a decade of FSLN-controlled terror and three decades of Cuban-backed terrorism. So extensive have these deceptions been that it would take a separate study to document the extent of Sandinista subterfuge on this aspect of their international relations. Indeed, except for the Nandaime episode on July 10, 1988, the extent of FSLN involvement in genocidal war, terrorism, and outlawry, and its support of national liberation fronts through the clandestine supply of arms across international frontiers, has resulted in only minor condemnation of FSLN actions since they seized power in 1979.[29]

The Soviets have even been more successful in this deception game, by masking their involvement in fueling wars of national liberation, and in disguising their disinterest in the soft underbelly of the United States. In an interview in early 1983, for example, Yuri Andropov drew an analogy between Afghanistan and Nicaragua, suggesting that because of Central America's geographic proximity, Nicaragua was in the United States' "sphere of influence" much as Afghanistan was in the Soviet sphere.[30] Even as late as February 1987, Boris Yeltsin, then Moscow's Party chief, assured leaders of Nicaragua's internal opposition parties that "Moscow does not wish the Nicaraguan Revolution to be part of either the Soviet or the American bloc."[31]

While consolidation of the Sandinista regime must remain of real concern to U.S. national-security analysts, of equal concern must be the "prolonged war concept" being employed against El Salvador since the failure of the guerrilla offensive against that country in 1981. The Moscow-Cuba axis, which had played such a large role in bringing the Sandinistas to power, soon again encouraged the formation of a united front for early guerrilla operations against El Salvador. Thus, too, did Castro's DA assume its role in providing training and matériel with the formation of the Unified Revolutionary Directorate in May 1980, and with the unification of rival Marxist-Leninist factions later that year as the Farabundo Marti Liberation Front (FMLN), after Augustin Farabundo Marti, a Salvadoran Communist during the 1930s. Next, Managua became the center for the clandestine flow of arms and matériel because of its ideal location and secure communication links with El Salvador's FMLN. Vessels disguised as fishing boats would leave Nicaragua's northwestern coast and transfer arms to large motorized canoes plying the myriad bays and inlets of El Salvador's southern coastal region (see Appendix 1, Map 5). These arms continue to flow across the Gulf of Fonseca despite the hazards of capture and the large sum of contraband cargoes seized by Salvadoran authorities, as in the case of thirty-four such canoes captured in a single raid in May 1984.[32]

In short, fueling national liberation fronts represents an essential element of Soviet strategy in Central America. It is, of course, a recognized tenet of Leninist doctrine, and it explains why the Soviets have been successful in seizing the "strategic initiative," whereas the "democratic opposition" has not. The matter is of utmost seriousness, when one recalls the successful strategic initiative of the late 1950s and in the following era under détente, when the Moscow-Havana axis succeeded in fueling further insurgencies in the region. Therefore, as long as this ominous threat of expanded war in the region exists, there can be no doubt it will continue to affect, directly and indirectly, the security and national welfare of the other states in the region, including the United States. Bolaños Hunter and Miranda Bengoechea have equally sought to convey this fact to U.S. authorities and an attentive public. As Bolaños Hunter explains: "El Salvador is a test case. If they are successful, the Sandinistas will remove some of the pressure on themselves by surrounding Nicaragua with allies."[33] In the long run, should the Soviet Union succeed through such untenable means of drawing Nicaragua—not to mention El Salvador—into the Soviet bloc, the Soviet Union, through its Cuban satellite, will have achieved the greatest possible victory in its march toward world hegemony.

Soviet Aims Unmasked: An Appraisal

IDEOLOGY AND GEOSTRATEGIC AIMS

In theory, if not in fact, Moscow's Marxist–Leninists regard their regime as marking a new beginning for mankind. Henceforth, *Homo sapiens* is in the process of becoming *Homo sovieticus*, or Soviet man. Hence it did not matter that millions were sent to their death by this regime, since history will vindicate the revolution's sacrifices in creating Soviet man.[1] Hence, too, it did not matter that the new Soviet state rests on no recognizable legal foundation other than the ideology which sustains it. As for the West, in its lack of a determined commitment to freedom since 1917, the problem posed by the Soviet regime and its ideology remains unresolved. First the USSR was made to appear "progressive"; then it was made to appear as a "gallant ally" in fighting fascism and Nazism alongside the West; finally, except for a brief period after 1945, it was made to appear as a traditional state, neither worse nor better than its Western counterpart, and so as "morally equivalent."[2]

Only when Stalin tried to acquire new frontiers at the expense of the West did the latter act in self-defense; only then did the West perceive the real danger posed by Soviet expansionism in

Europe against "free peoples" and adopt a strategy of its own. Still, the consensus on the issue of Soviet expansionism began to lose ground following the Cuban missile crisis of 1962, when Moscow withdrew its nuclear missiles from Cuba, and as U.S. policymakers began to yield to a policy of accommodation and then détente with the USSR between 1969 and 1979.[3] Nonetheless, the effort to "socialize" the Soviets and assuage their fears through commercial, financial, and disarmament accords came to naught, since Soviet ideology and Soviet foreign policy are fatally linked. Indeed, the détente era marked a retreat from strategic reality, as the rival to the United States sought to reduce U.S. power in Latin America by substituting its own, wherever and whenever possible.[4]

In truth, Soviet leaders can no more abandon their foreign policy than they can abandon the military state that supports it. Only defeat might do that by forcing their elite to look inward as a result rather than continuing to look outward. So the party *nomenklatura* must continue to expand its power in the face of rival power, however benign the latter's intentions, or face the prospect of its own demise as a consequence of its failure to expand. So Arkady Shevchenko, Moscow's highest-ranking defector, also concludes: "As long as the *nomenklatura* remains what it is, as long as the Soviet Union lives in a state of lawlessness, as long as the energies of its peoples are not allowed to express themselves . . . there can be no security for anyone else in the world."[5]

So it has been since 1945, when the Soviet elite under Stalin's tutelage declared World War III against their new archenemy and custodian of the wartime Western coalition: the United States. Indeed, in June 1945, a U.S. intelligence officer then in Moscow, James G. McCargar, was obliged to report on this new war in the making to his superiors in Washington.[6] Stalin, moreover, lost no time in linking foreign policy to Soviet actions on three fronts. One front envisaged probing Western strategic positions to determine "how far" Soviet gains could be advanced without risking open warfare with the West. A second marked the resumption of secret operations "to reduce the advantages of Western technology" along with the resumption of "political and psychological warfare." The third, and doubtless most important front in shaping Soviet foreign policy after 1945, was Lenin's plan of attacking imperialism at its "weakest link," in Asia, Africa, and Latin America. Inaugurated at the Second Congress of the Communist International in 1920, Lenin's plan became the "theoretical foundation" for the liberation fronts that Stalin first sought to promote throughout Latin America in the 1920s and 1930s. Then, too, began the effort found indispensable later in the development of subversive tactics, including the most easily usable, anti-Yankeeism; still, local issues were also exploited as tactical means for "boring from within," as Lenin advocated. Such issues were the peasants' hunger for land, labor-management frictions, and poverty itself.[7] Thence followed, after Stalin's passing and the abortive attempt to install a Marxist-Leninist regime in Guatemala in 1954, the most important tactics or principles devised for seizing and holding power. Indeed, the lessons learned from that failure have proved to be decisive ever since.

Accordingly, it was the Guatemalan Communist party's Central Committee that drew up six basic principles to account for its failure to achieve power in 1954. The six principles, it should be underscored, guided both the Castroites and the Sandinistas in seizing power in 1959 and 1979. Above all, the lessons of failure in Guatemala learned by the Communists were equalled only by the failure of U.S. policymakers to learn from their success in 1954. Finally, these controlling principles assume a historical importance second only to the overall character and focus of Soviet foreign policy in the region since that time.[8]

One principle held that, while the middle class was needed to attain power, only by revolutionizing the masses could power be retained. The second was equally important in holding that "political rights" can only be exercised by the "vanguard," or Communist party, to the exclusion of all others; third, that "the Church must be broken or discredited in order to eliminate a rallying point for anti-Communists"; fourth, that the army of the old regime must be replaced by the revolution's own cadres; fifth, that "all appeals should be made to the United Nations, where the Soviet Union sits on the Security Council"; and sixth, that Communist states in the Americas must integrate economically with the Soviet bloc in order to reduce their dependence on the United States.[9] It was only the last principle that was later modified, since Castro's retaliation against U.S. interests in Cuba, economic and then diplomatic, early deprived Cuba of U.S. trade and access to U.S. capital.[10]

Strategically, the Cuban missile crisis of 1962 also taught Moscow's leaders some valuable lessons. It showed them that superior sea power combined with a nuclear weapons advantage of 8 to 1, and possibly as high as 10 to 1, gave the United States an unmatched advantage—one that could have been turned to greater advantage by demanding more. Accordingly, the Soviets moved quickly to build a massive nuclear ballistic missile program, much as they responded earlier on learning that the United States had produced its first atomic weapons in 1945. As a result, by 1969 the Soviets had achieved parity with the United States in nuclear missile capability, and parallel to that had moved to accelerate their naval construction program started in 1959. In reality, then, the Cuban missile crisis served to magnify Soviet aims in the Caribbean—a region that had been safe for U.S. commerce and investment since the Spanish-American War— through their military buildup in Cuba to unprecedented levels. Instead of moving in step with U.S. policy by showing like restraint and accommodation, the Soviets exercised the option of increasing their naval and political presence in the region between 1969 and the overthrow of Somoza's government in 1979, the same years now regarded as the era of détente. In fact, according to a staff member of the Senate Foreign Relations Committee, the Soviet "threat from Cuba . . . is more than twice what it was during the Cuban missile crisis . . ." since Moscow has attained a 4-to-1 advantage in ICBM delivery capability, and insofar as Cuba has been turned into a major Soviet strategic base.[11]

The confrontation that created the Cuban missile crisis has thus brought to the fore the nature of Soviet geostrategic aims in the region. Indeed, whatever the qualms of geographers, political scientists, and historians involving geopolitical theories, it is apparent that the Soviets are attempting to intrude *militarily* beyond Cuba and across the United States's southern flank in the Caribbean.

Incrementally, then, encirclement, isolation, and denial could result from the Soviet Union's ability to project its military power in the region through its clandestine policies of subversion and in pressing its newfound advantage in strategic, naval, and nuclear capability by enveloping the southern flank. This "grand design" is strikingly reminiscent of the maritime strategy that England pursued against Spain in the seventeenth century.[12] Unlike England's New World strategy, however, when oil and ore were not essential commodities, these resources have become the life-blood of the industrialized world. Consequently, their denial would contribute in the long run to "the destruction of the economic base of the United States and its Western allies. . . ."[13] Geostrategically, then, and in defiance of geographic proximity and of U.S. national "self-defense" policy invoked in 1917 and in 1940,[14] the Soviets seek to replace U.S. interests with their own. If such aims are not defeated, Soviet strategy could indeed lead to isolation and denial, and, ultimately, to the defeat of U.S. interests and security, including access to oil and ore resources that pass through the Caribbean to U.S. gulf coast ports (see Appendix 1, Map 6).

Encirclement, or envelopment, of the United States would be markedly advanced by the Soviet satellization of Nicaragua. Since Nicaragua occupies a strategic position on the land bridge between North and South America, as a garrison state allied to the Soviet Union and Cuba, Nicaragua would eventually erode the national will of the surrounding states, resulting either in their subjection or accommodation to Nicaragua's overriding influence. The example of Nazi expansionism in the 1930s serves as a forceful reminder of this process of envelopment, as does the mind-set of appeasement of that era. "Did little bits and pieces of Europe . . . really matter? Could or should we risk peace in our time? History clearly demonstrates what the answer should have been but was not."[15] The aim of Soviet foreign policy in the post-Stalinist period has followed this geostrategic line of advance. The issue is obvious. Policymakers understand the importance of maintaining the regional balance of power. How long, then, could U.S. policymakers countenance a shift in the balance of power that would result if Nicaragua becomes, in toto, another Communist state?

Lastly, as part of this appraisal of Soviet aims, a key question concerns whether needed Soviet domestic changes will tend to moderate the USSR's expansionist aims under Mikhail Gorbachev, since the old guard is also relinquishing power. Indeed, since coming to power in 1985, following Konstantine Chernenko's brief tenure, Gorbachev has made promises of reform that have only heightened such speculation. In contrast to détente, for example, Gorbachev's promises of *perestroika* (restructuring) and *glasnost* (openness) represent a reversal of Soviet domestic policy. That is, détente was intended to prevent domestic reforms, whereas perestroika and glasnost are intended to promote them.[16] Significantly, there are three reasons for this reversal. One is the severe food crisis that is again reaching epidemic proportions. Even sugar is rationed, not to mention meat and butter in several of the USSR's major cities. The second reason is due to the resurgence of nationalism, as in the formerly independent Baltic states. The third flows from both these reasons insofar as economic reform also aims at mitigating the food crisis and in stemming the tide of nationalist discontent.[17] Shevchenko wrote, as the Chernenko regime was being replace by Gorbachev's, that the new regime might begin to pay some attention to another Marxist-Leninist idea—namely, "that socialism should [also] serve as an inspiring example of domestic performance to other peoples. . . ."[18]

In consequence, the impact of these improvements or changes internally on Soviet expansionist aims can only be regarded as limiting Soviet economic assistance to Nicaragua, but not in limiting continued military aid to the Sandinistas.[19] In that respect, perestroika and glasnost mark a "breathing spell" for Soviet planners while the Soviet elite regroups. Accordingly, Gorbachev's promises, if successful, can be expected to stabilize Moscow's internal problems, reduce tensions, and give the people new hope, while at the same time strengthening the USSR's position with its Third World and potential Third World clients.[20] Looked at in retrospect, Gorbachev's policies are reminiscent of the early post-Stalin years, when Stalin's inheritors were contending with inertia and with symptoms of internal malaise. Then, too, they relaxed controls over the arts and literature, emphasized a "new course" in economic policy on the consumer front, and showed a new moderation, if only deceptively so, in signing the Austrian State Treaty (1955), thereby relinquishing their occupation zone in Austria. Thereafter, as soon as the regime regrouped and was again in full control, it reverted to its previous domestic stance and resumed its expansionism abroad.[21]

The Grasp for World Power

During the decade of the 1980s, and perhaps even more pronounced than at any time since 1945, Soviet foreign policy has been guided by three components, or strategies, corresponding to policy initiatives in the military, economic, and political realms. Above all, in the military realm, the Soviets have continued to pursue a policy of "military superiority" over the West, while at the same time trying to moderate Western military outlays through the skillful use of propaganda in support of "the peace movement." Thus does the Soviet Union's military buildup continue under Gorbachev; thus, too, does Moscow sustain "militarily the lines of communication" with its client-states in Cuba and Nicaragua. And in the broader realm of military policy and strategy, Soviet military superiority is used to impress other peoples, notably in the Third World, with its superpower role in order to "support Soviet claims and interests in every region of the world, however remote." Finally, Soviet might serves to divert the attention of its own peoples from their daily economic and social problems by emphasizing the USSR's "status as a world power."[22] Similarly, in the economic realm, Moscow seeks to expand its economic ties with the West to promote its foreign policy aims. Although Gorbachev's reform policies under perestroika and glasnost are doubtless genuine, in contrast to détente, they are nonetheless designed to attract "business circles" to support policies conducive to cooperation with the Soviet Union for the financing of "construction projects" on a long-term basis, and so they resemble détente for that reason. Lastly, in the political realm, Soviet aims are advanced "by adroitly exploiting differences of opinion," by dealing separately with Western states, and by attempting to sow disunity in their ranks, and among contending political groups and their constituents in the West generally.[23]

At issue, then, are the main reasons behind Soviet planning and decision making in its military, political, and economic assault on the West—and, above all, in Moscow's planning and decision making in its assault on the United States's southern flank. To reiterate, the overall reasons are two: because the United States is the world power that stands in the way of Soviet hegemonic aims, and because the Caribbean and Central America are the United States's soft underbelly and imperialism's weakest link. Hence, having strategic allies as Cuba and Nicaragua on the southern flank is essential to advancing Moscow's hegemonic aims and in weakening the United States. On the other hand, without the military power and weaponry to hold these strategic allies in place, Moscow's entire Caribbean strategy would collapse.

Geostrategically, the two systems are on a collision course, not because the United States is unable to live with the Soviet Union, but because the latter is unable to coexist with the West. The party *nomenklatura* cannot coexist with the West and still hope to perpetuate itself. To recall, the Soviet power elite must continue to expand its power or perish. The Soviet elite also fears that Third World countries will take "the Japanese path" and not the "Cuban path," and thereby strengthen the Western system even more.[24]

In conclusion, Soviet expansionism in the Caribbean and Central America has come to dominate Soviet strategic planning and geostrategic policy, even though their planning and policy continues to serve their expansionist aims worldwide.[25] Likewise, though the six principles of 1954 continue to guide and inform the insurgency movements inside Central America, it is still Soviet and Soviet bloc military aid that sustains Cuban-Nicaraguan expansionism in the region. Consequently, only by showing that insurgency movements can fail can the United States hope to blunt continued Soviet interventionist aims in the region, and ultimately to force Moscow to look inward by granting its people the post-détente policies necessary to break up the power elite and its absolute monopoly over Soviet foreign policy. So the main purpose of a "Western counterstrategy should be to compel the Soviet Union to turn inward—from foreign conquest to reform."[26] Only by defeating such aims, and the purpose of organizing yet another insurgency into becoming another "strategic ally," can U.S. policymakers hope to deter and eventually defeat Soviet-Cuban interventionist policy in the Americas.[27] Indeed, so important is this task for U.S. national security, that it must be made a principal objective of an enlightened U.S. Latin American policy in the years ahead. Only through its accomplishment can the United States hope to end World War III, by forcing Moscow to turn inward and undertake genuine measures conducive to real reform. Only then will Soviet geostrategic aims be diverted from their present course in the Soviet quest for world hegemony.

Averting Checkmate:
"Western Strategy" Reconsidered

BEYOND THE REAGAN DOCTRINE?

Between 1954 and 1984, the United States succeeded in protecting its interests and that of its Caribbean neighbors on two further occasions: in 1965 with respect to the Dominican Republic and in 1983 with respect to Grenada. These defensive successes, however, must be measured against the dramatic failures of U.S. policy in 1959, in failing to protect Cuba from Communist subversion, and again in 1979, in failing to protect Nicaragua from a similar fate. How then could it be, after four years of Sandinista rule and in the aftermath of Grenada's liberation, that Washington did not also find it politically necessary to act with firmness and dispatch against the Marxist-Leninist regime of Nicaragua? How could it be that fifteen more months would pass before the president would announce the Reagan Doctrine before a joint session of the Congress? Perhaps only future historians will be able to answer such questions satisfactorily.[1]

Thus, by 1983, when the United States had provided aid to the resistance in Nicaragua for the first time, U.S. assistance totaling

$24 million was dwarfed by the more than $400 million in military aid alone that the Soviet Union had provided the Sandinistas up to that time.[2] But more important even than the aid itself was the Soviet resolve in demonstrating once more that its aim in Central America had nothing to do with an "altruistic desire" to replace the discredited Somoza regime with one pledged to building socialism. That is, the only reason for Soviet interest in Nicaragua, as in Cuba, is its geostrategic location; hence the importance of both countries as strategic assets and not otherwise. Strategically, then, Nicaragua augurs to become another asset within 500 miles of the Panama Canal, and the Soviets are allegedly training some 10,000 people (mostly Panamanians) to operate the canal when the United States turns over the Canal Zone to Panama under the Carter-Torrijos treaties by the year 2000[3] (see Appendix 1, Map 2). The author of an important study regarding Soviet strategic interests in the region concludes: "Were this not the case, it is highly unlikely that the economically troubled USSR would continue subsidizing the Castro regime."[4] And this is equally true of Nicaragua, although the Soviets have been pressing the FSLN to look for other sources of support on the economic front, in line with the aforementioned revision made in the six principles since 1961.[5]

When the Reagan Doctrine was finally launched in the president's State of the Union Address in February 1985, it was couched in language reminiscent of the Truman Doctrine of global containment, though President Reagan did stress the "self-defense" nature of what the freedom fighters represented, and that this principle was "totally consistent with the OAS and U.N. Charters."[6] What seemed missing were the broader implications of what this new policy actually constituted, not in ideological terms but militarily, economically, politically, and socially. To be sure, the Nicaraguan freedom fighters were acting in their own self-defense, but they were also acting in accordance with U.S. defense and in support of the internationally recognized principle of national self-determination.

One of the difficulties that has plagued U.S. foreign policy since the mid–1950s has been the failure to incorporate the lessons of the Guatemalan success story of 1954 into later formulations of U.S. national security policy. Why this did not occur and why the Inter-American Defense Board (IADB) did not assume an increasingly important role in overseeing hemispheric defense is an important subject in itself. Suffice here to note only that U.S. national security policy tended to place Central America on the periphery in the rank-ordering of foreign policy concerns, beneath the Soviet Union and Western Europe, as well as beneath the Middle East, Japan, and East Asia.[7] This ordering of foreign policy concerns tended to sacrifice legitimate hemispheric defense to the all-encompassing needs of the containment theory in an effort to halt Soviet expansionism. The theory of containment worked well when it was limited to Western Europe, but it was of less relevance in the Third World, where few governments, especially in Latin America until the 1980s, could be defined as democratic. This distinction is important to understanding the limits of containment; it is necessary only to recall the collapse of U.S. security policy in failing to support Batista in 1958 and the Somoza regime in 1978. True, neither country was democratic in the traditional sense, but both regimes were pro–U.S. and both for that reason stood as a bulwark against Soviet subversion in the region.

No longer should there be any confusion as to what the Reagan Doctrine is about, even though it resembles the Truman Doctrine in its ideological aspects. Thus its focus is not Europe-centered but Third World–centered.[8] Lastly, the criticism that the Reagan Doctrine was too ideologically oriented could have been avoided if Reagan officials had spoken with one voice concerning the strategic threat to the southern flank, and had emphasized why continued aid to the Nicaraguan resistance remained essential to achieving eventual national reconciliation and peace.[9]

In 1962, the late Senator Thomas Dodd of Connecticut urged that the United States commit itself to a "declaration of freedom for the Cuban people" by recognizing a provisional Cuban government in exile. Perhaps that advice ought to serve as a reminder to policymakers today, and that U.S. leaders ought to give serious consideration to this possibility in the case of Nicaragua.[10] A broadly representative Nicaraguan government in exile, backed by U.S. support, might well be the first step in breathing new life into the Reagan Doctrine. Still, other measures must be considered if it should not prove feasible to reconstitute the Nicaraguan resistance, including the revitalization of the IADB and its possible relocation from Washington, D.C., to Panama. If, however, the IADB cannot be revitalized because of current distrust of U.S. foreign policy on issues affecting the peace and security of the Western Hemisphere—the mission of the IADB—then U.S. policymakers will be faced with the more fundamental and formidable task of either establishing a new mechanism for ensuring peace and security as a hemispheric goal or face the equally difficult task of dispelling the issue of distrust that currently prevails in U.S.–Latin American relations as a precondition of revitalizing the IADB.[11] Lastly, the establishment of the Special Operations Forces (SOF), with its own unified command under the National Defense Authorization Act of 1987, marks an important step in the right direction. Although belatedly created, establishment of SOF recognizes the nation's vulnerability to the threat of insurgency-terrorist warfare waged with Soviet-Cuban support inside Central America as a threat to U.S. security as well.[12]

To pretend otherwise—to act as though the United States is not in fact vulnerable to this intrusive threat through Central America—would be the height of folly. The authors of a special report on *State-Sponsored Terrorism* conclude: "This issue will not go away. . . . U.S. national security authorities will simply have to do a better educational job in delineating the Soviet . . . challenge and getting the Congress to recognize the strategic responsibilities" it has toward its constituents, toward the "general welfare," and toward the survival of the U.S. political system.[13]

In sum, it is the commitment to the principles of free society that must be nurtured and promoted if national self-determination is to prevail, if the democracies in the region are to develop and prosper, and if democratic principles are to be made secure against the inroads of opposing regimes that seek its destruction.

A Strategy of Survival

Brian Crozier was surely right when he wrote toward the end of the last decade that the time for "compromise and evasion is over."[14] That statement is even more true today than it was in 1978, the year before the overthrow of yet another government in the Caribbean basin.

World War III has been like no other world war in history. It has been a war that cannot be waged, as in World Wars I and II, in the open and across frontiers. Instead, it is waged by means of terror, subversion, and what has duly become known as wars of national liberation. All of these means have become a mask for Soviet strategic aggression against the West, and against the United States in particular. It seems odd, then, that U.S. leaders, even President Reagan himself, should have waited so long before responding to this growing threat to U.S. interests and security in Central America. In fact, by 1983, Nicaragua had already begun to take on the characteristics of a strategic asset of ominous potential in the next phase planned in the conduct of Soviet foreign policy in the Americas. Again, the nature of this threat, and its implications for U.S. security, must be fully recognized if a counterrevolutionary strategy is to be successfully forged. Only then can a U.S. counterstrategy be expected to be understood and supported; only then can it safely invoke the right of national self-defense in mobilizing American opinion against outside aggression under Article 51 of the United Nations Charter and Article 3 of the RIO Treaty. Only then, possibly, will U.S. neighbors perceive not weakness but resolve, and consistency instead of irresolution.

Last, and like Crozier's earlier statement, former U.S. Ambassador Lewis Tambs was surely right when he stated that the Reagan Doctrine gives the West "the opportunity to reverse the domino theory, a process by which the Soviet Union has sought since 1917 and increasingly since 1945 to . . . achieve global domination by promoting terrorism, insurgency and subversion."[15] Such a strategy, he explains, must incorporate two major goals for the region if it is to be successful: peace and national reconciliation. Accordingly, with a consensus on the essentials of policy and strategy in place, these goals, he averred, can best be attained through the adoption of a five-point program: defense, including defense of the United States and its neighbors in Central America; democracy; development; demilitarization; and the departure of foreign forces.[16]

The end result of such a concerted and coordinated strategy, and if implemented with dispatch, would signal a decisive blow to Soviet strategic aims in the region. Coupled with increasing pressure for real reform, such an outcome would likely force Moscow to turn inward to address domestic needs, and thereby doom any further prospects for Soviet expansion in the hemisphere. It may not be quite in the same category as Charles Martel, who allegedly saved Christianity from the infidel, though the parallels would not be inappropriate. And such an outcome would ensure the future and growth of free society; in all likelihood, likewise, it would doom the hideous experiment to create Soviet man. Lastly, such an outcome would also mark the terminal phase of World War III.

Appendix I: Maps

NOTES ON MAPS

Map 1. Nicaragua is roughly the size of Michigan, and is strategically located on the isthmus between Honduras to the north and Costa Rica to the south. Assuming its feasibility, any projected canal would follow the San Juan River from San Juan del Norte on the Caribbean to Lake Nicaragua, and thence to the Pacific in the vicinity of San Juan del Sur.

Map 2. Nicaragua is some 900 miles from southernmost Florida and about 1,000 miles from the Texas border. Nicaragua's population is about 3 million.

Map 3. Depicted are the seven refugee camps as of 1983–84, showing five in Honduras and two in Costa Rica.

Map 4. Depicts the very rapid military buildup under the new regime, made possible by Soviet and Soviet bloc support before any counterinsurgency movement existed.

Map 5. Exhibited are the principal land and sea routes for supplying guerrilla operations against El Salvador's government, showing that the bulk of the arms and supplies to the Salvadoran guerrillas are funneled by sea from Nicaragua.

Map 6. Illustrates the importance of America's southern flank to U.S. trade, to the flow of vital ore and oil, and to the resupply of NATO forces in the event of hostilities.

Map 1
Nicaragua's Location in Central America

Source: Central Intelligence Agency.

Map 2

Nicaragua's Distance Relative to North America and Its Population

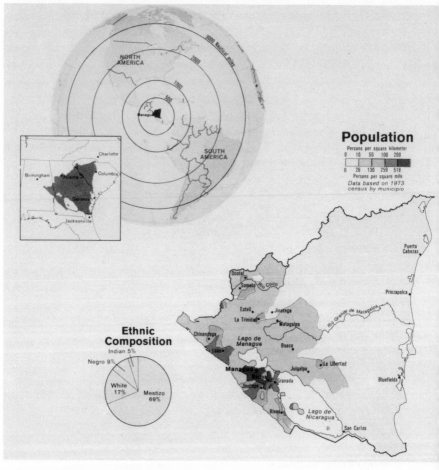

Source: Central Intelligence Agency.

Map 3
Refugee Flow from Nicaragua and Neighboring El Salvador

CENTRAL AMERICA
MAJOR REFUGEE FLOWS AND SETTLEMENTS
(DECEMBER 1983)

Source: General Accounting Office, Report to the Congress by the Comptroller General, *Central American Refugees: Regional Conditions and Prospects and Potential Impact on the United States* (1984).

Map 4
The Sandinista Military Buildup

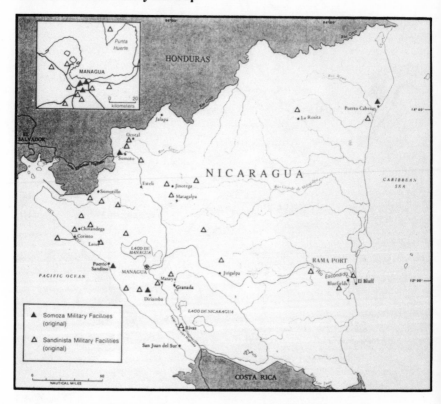

Source: Department of State and Department of Defense, *The Sandinista Military Build-up* (Inter-American Series, 1985).

Map 5

Nicaragua's Support of Insurgency Against El Salvador

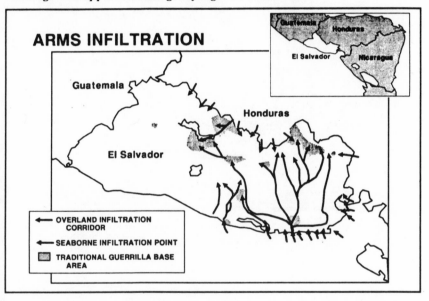

Source: Department of State and Department of Defense, *The Soviet-Cuban Connection in Central America and the Caribbean* (1985).

Map 6
Regional Map with Strategic Data

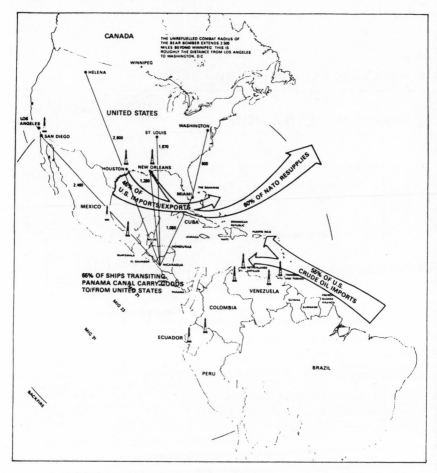

Source: Department of Defense, *Soviet Bloc Military Equipment Supplied to Nicaragua, July 1979–October 1987, Graphic Supplement* (1987).

Appendix 2

DRAFT OF "1988 STRATEGY"

The following document was released for internal review on March 28, 1988. That it was drafted about this time is also apparent from the reference on page 86, where reference is made to the scheduled delivery of Soviet arms shipments "for the first months of this year" (1988), and that such deliveries have "already started." Marked "Secret," the document provides an inside view of how the Sandinista leaders view themselves, their internal opponents, the Nicaraguan resistance, their neighbors, and, above all, the United States, relative to their domestic and foreign policy strategy. Indeed, as "confiscated power" can only be maintained through force and intimidation, consistent elements throughout the document, and corresponding to Marxist-Leninist regimes generally, point to the document's authenticity.

Lastly, there are a few places where the text was not translatable. But for these omissions, and the two appendices to this protocol mentioned therein, the document appears in its entirety in English from an original draft in Spanish of the Frente Sandinista's "1988 Strategy."

DRAFT
Judicial Record 1740
Extraordinary Session No. 47
"1988 STRATEGY"

Against the [omission], the strategy to follow in search of a critical route, among the obstacles placed on this road, which will allow us to maintain both the power and the revolutionary project.

Such critical route should help us face successfully the difficulties of the international conjuncture which is composed of the consequences of the Esquipulas II pact, the imperialist pressure, and the status of the revolutionary struggle in Central America; as well as the problems caused by the internal conjuncture, such as the serious economic crisis, the intensified counterrevolutionary attacks, the cease-fire negotiations, the increasing popular uneasiness, and the consolidation of the domestic opposition.

The decisions made in relation to both conjunctures are summarized as follows:

INTERNAL CONJUNCTURE

1. Economic Crisis

The economic crisis will be confronted by a New Economic Policy that will allow us to regain spaces and to consolidate the revolutionary victories. In order to put them into practice, the following policies should be in effect:

a. The hyperinflationary process must be halted completely by means of a new monetary reform, which has been already discussed and approved. In order to consolidate this economic adjustment in a short term, it will be up to the revolutionary government to rigorously apply extra economic positions [omission] of the popular organizations.

b. Public expenses should be drastically reduced and reassigned with partisan criteria. This reduction will be accomplished in the context of a military confrontation with imperialism that we will study in detail later. The work-force reduction will be done strictly on partisan criteria.

c. Reactivate both the state and private productions, according to the plan presented by Comrade Luis Carrión, and modifications suggested by Comrade Henry Ruiz. Until further authorization, confiscation of properties and goods are not in order.

d. Owing to the fact that the concerns of our strategic ally, the Soviet Union, are mainly concentrated on the geopolitical problems generated by the world struggle against imperialism, rather than acting in solidarity with the Revolution (although this idea is not shared by all attendants), we should expect that their military aid will continue to arrive according to our needs, but we should not expect the same on the economic assistance that we need so urgently.

Under this assumption, we will try to obtain external financial resources from the European Economic Community (EEC) countries. With this purpose, we will provide complete support to the plan presented by Comrade Gabriel Siry and the suggestions made by Marco Villamar of SIECA (these documents are presented as Appendices A and B of this Protocol), which are based on the possibility of taking advantage of the astringency of North American aid to the region, the urgent needs of the Central American countries, the multilateral actions and exploitation of some protagonist desires of some European countries in Latin America, which emanate from the contradictions of the capitalistic system.

2. Domestic Policy

a. Military sector.

The key assignment of the Dirección Nacional is, at this moment, the strategic defeat of the counterrevolution. The accomplishment of this goal will define in a great deal our survival, consolidation, and advancement of our historic project. In order to reach these goals, we will take the following steps:

—Prevent, by any means, the approval of any additional aid to the counterrevolution by the North American Congress, taking advantage of the Reagan administration's final stage, and the disagreements between Republicans and Democrats that have increased during the electoral campaign.

The key element of our campaign will be the promise to comply with the peace plan of Esquipulas II. Like the Vietnam War, we will win this war in Washington by providing all required resources for the lobby and by not carrying out any act that may modify the majority vote of the Congress. Now is the time to reactivate protests by the solidarity committees throughout the United States.

—Once this goal has been achieved, we will proceed to cut every access of the counterrevolution to their sanctuaries in Honduras, even if this means creating border incidents. This will be accomplished in the context of a general offensive.

As the Honduran military has shown previously, they fear that a disbandment of the mercenaries without imperialist support will create a serious military problem, which could jeopardize the Army's superiority.

On the other hand, they question the imperialist commitment to defend them, therefore they feel they are at the mercy of our military superiority.

The purpose of creating border incidents is to give the Honduran government a chance to eliminate the counterrevolutionaries, and to accept a U.N. vigilance commission that will assure a clean northern border.

At the same time, a general military offensive against the counterrevolutionary forces will be launched in order to disband them and to destroy their logistic supplies network.

In order to accomplish these assignments we need to fortify the EPS military doctrine, to increase the military draft, and to increase troop morale.

The arrival of armaments from the Soviet Union required to reaffirm our technological military superiority is scheduled for the first months of this year, and it has already started.

b. Domestic opposition and reactionary dissatisfaction.

The political concessions we have been forced to make in order to demonstrate to the international forum that we are complying with the Esquipulas II treaty, especially the reopening of *La Prensa* and independent radio-news stations, the lifting of the State of Emergency, the economic crisis, and the reappearance of partisan structures, have all contributed to the flourishing of dissatisfaction from some popular sectors that are not in agreement with the revolutionary process.

The combination of the freedom given to the ideological enemies that are in charge of the media and the popular dissatisfaction has a highly explosive potential against the revolutionary power. It is a high-priority assignment, therefore, to reduce and control the popular dissatisfaction to a level where we can still manage our external image.

Our policy should be oriented to prevent the utilization of this dissatisfaction by our enemies from both domestic and external opposition, so they could not take advantage of that political space that has been granted. For this, the following will be required:

—to reinforce the organization of masses, especially the CDS.

—to restructure the judicial system.

—to control the popular dissatisfaction by the utilization of armed organization of masses.

—to control the leadership of the opposition by strict vigilance and personal intimidation.

—to mobilize our supporters so we can negate the streets to opposition.

The limits of the internal political space that is required in order to pretend that we are complying with Esquipulas II will be totally defined, taking advantage of the general military offensive and the border occurrences provoked. Our troop incursions in Honduras in pursuit of mercenaries will more likely prompt an imperialist reaction, which should be handled carefully but without fear. We will take advantage of them by overexciting both their nationalism and their anti-imperialism in order to mobilize the people and to adjust the political space to the proper dimensions, and also to regain our anti-imperialist position in Europe and Latin America.

Another important problem we must solve is the strong tendency of unification that exists in the 14 political parties of the internal reaction, and also its political coordination with the counterrevolution which has been noticeable from the beginning of the year.

Even with the efforts we have made to keep the domestic opposition divided and controlled, we must accept that we have failed to do so, and that renewed efforts are required in order to accomplish such goal. This is an extremely important assignment, since we cannot allow an opposition that is unified and coordinated with the counterrevolution, especially now with the ceasefire negotiations and internal and external "democratization" demands.

We will be frank with the reactionaries on this point, and we will make every effort in order to divide and dissolve them. We cannot, at this point, ignore the use of revolutionary terror.

The limits of tolerance of the internal opposition's activities will be determined by making an offer to the leadership that should be based on a privilege quota rather than a power quota—all of this in order to obtain legitimacy in the process.

The arrival to the country of Comrade Eden Pastora will be to our advantage in order to divide and confuse the reactionary ranks.

c. Cease-Fire negotiations.

These conversations should have as framework the general military offensive, the adjustment of the internal political space, and the new economic order.

Our representation during the negotiations will be adequately handled according to the current perspectives. Comrade Humberto Ortega Saavedra will make the final decision on this subject.

The National Reconciliation Commission, using our veto power, will be momentarily frozen.

The revolutionary constitutional order will never be broken and will be the frame of reference on every agreement.

We will, at the proper time, eliminate Obando as mediator, not allowing him to resign; in return, we will augment our representation at the highest level and we will propose direct negotiations on Nicaraguan soil. Obando will always be our enemy, and it is not to our advantage to maintain him as mediator.

In order to manage the negotiations, we will act according to the following guidelines:

We will not negotiate with the counterrevolution, but with the Reagan administration.

We will not negotiate a democratization that already exists; we will only talk of the cease-fire technical aspects described in our proposal.

The political internal space required to incorporate the counterrevolutionaries with the civic opposition and to abandon their arms already exists.

The Nicaraguan people is the Sandinista people, who are totally integrated with the FSLN vanguard.

We should keep the dynamic of the concessions in our favor, so we can participate in the negotiations with strength.

Amnesty to the genocide army and counterrevolution would be guaranteed only if they leave the country; otherwise the people would murder them in the streets.

If conditions allow it, and before the talks begin, some "democratization" measures will be taken in order to disarm the counterrevolution demands; this will prevent them from summoning us to comply and it will center the negotiation on whether or not we will comply, therefore extending the talks indefinitely.

We will only hold negotiations on "democratization" with the domestic opposition, once we have them divided and the counterrevolution has been weakened.

For the cease-fire negotiations, it would be advisable to have the secretary of the Organization of American States (OAS) participate, since he recently requested our support for his re-election. This support will be conditioned on a favorable participation.

EXTERNAL CONJUNCTURE

1. The Consequences of Esquipulas II

Thus far, the revolutionary leadership has been able to handle the consequences of Esquipulas II successfully. This successful operation allowed [us] to mock the maneuvers of the Central American reaction that, in conjunction with the imperialist pressures, attempted to put the Revolution in a straitjacket. On the contrary, taking advantage of the tensions between U.S. Imperialism and Latin America, we have been able to accomplish the opposite, since at this time the ones who are really in a straitjacket and have placed themselves in the defendant's bench are the Central American oligarchic governments.

By mid–1987, when we notified Costa Rican President Oscar Arias on the Frente Sandinista's desire to support a Costa Rican initiative to pacify Central America, and on our willingness to make some substantial concessions, the Dirección Nacional's definite intention was to create a proper framework to consolidate the Revolution and its accomplishments. At that time, we considered appropriate that the gains had been sufficient, and that it was the time to stop and evaluate in order to secure positions that later would allow us to go forward.

Today Esquipulas II has created proper conditions for the consolidation of the process and revolutionary gains in Central America, since, while on one hand it allows us to neutralize and dismantle the enemies of the Revolution, on the other it weakens reactionary positions in the other Central American countries, which are being confronted by popular sectors based on "democratization" demands.

Esquipulas II granted legitimacy to the Revolutionary Government, which has been questioned after the 1984 elections in Nicaragua, and also recognized the validity of our constitution at an international level.

Once these two basic points have been consolidated, we should only need to carefully manage in order to control our concessions and prove them properly before international public opinion.

The "wealthy" leadership in Central America is weak, unstable, and corrupt; it is willing to accept a minimum and even symbolic compliance with the treaties in order to get some peace that allows it to continue to enjoy its profits and power.

Based on the current situation, and as long as we can keep the army, the party, and the mass organizations, we can afford the luxury of letting the wealthy middle-class opposition manage part of the public administration, so they would take responsibility of the economic crisis and its costs. We will never allow them, however, to take control of the real power structure. There is in Nicaragua an established revolutionary system that must be respected and defended with all available means, including revolutionary violence.

In its time Esquipulas II has been favorable to us in every one of its aspects:

The mandate to suspend aid to irregular forces has been a key element to leave the counterrevolution with no resources.

Simultaneity and verification will allow us to demand from Honduras that it stop being a counterrevolutionary sanctuary.

The ceasefire will accelerate the mercenary forces' disarmament and surrender.

The "democratization" and "reconciliation" will provide for the cooperation of the main groups of the wealthy opposition, forcing them to accept our system and to maintain their activities within the revolutionary legality.

Owing to the access to the media that we have allowed our enemies, and the drastic opening of the political space after lifting the State of Emergency, we are aware of the serious problem we now face; and we are convinced that we should confront them with patience and make use of the fist of popular power against the abuses of the reactionaries.

2. The Imperialist Pressure

The "paper tiger" (as Comrade Mao wisely called North American imperialism) has defined its policy toward the Revolution as pressure to put us back on democratic routes. Although in a different context this definition should not be believed, the truth is that imperialism has remained without options in the revolutionary advance in Central America.

The multiple syndromes affecting that society in decadence, after being defeated by the one thousand times heroic people of Vietnam, have generated the loss of national consensus and the distortion of national values. We ought to add to this the problems of conjuncture that have ruined the so-called Conservative Revolution of the Reagan administration, especially the failure of the economic policy and the existence of a parallel power centered on the Democratic wing of the Congress and headed by Jim Wright, which is constantly challenging the president's authority. The existence of this parallel power has indeed allowed us to tie the administration's hands in its attempt against the revolutionary process. The IRAN-CONTRA scandal, originated by the confrontation between the parties, has weakened Reagan's authority and therefore taken away in a critical moment the resources that it had to attack the Revolution. This has allowed us to overcome a highly dangerous period that will conclude with the end of the Reagan administration and the beginning of the electoral campaign.

Because of this, it is very unlikely to expect direct action against us by imperialism during the next months. Even though the Republican party may stay in power, its new leader, George Bush (no more than a caricature of Reagan), could be easier to control by using the tensions with the parallel power.

In order to reestablish imperial-society syndromes and fears, we need to take the following actions:

Launch harassment operations against the North American military bases in Honduras and Panama. Declare all North American military engineers and advisers in all Central American countries as military targets. Because of these casualties, the Vietnam specter will reappear in the general imperial memory, with its associated effects.

Additionally, and in order to take the streets to protest and create awareness on any act against the Revolution, we will activate to its maximum potential the solidarity committee network we use in the United States.

3. Status of the Revolutionary Struggle in Central America

a. Guatemala.

Although a military coup is very unlikely, the local conjuncture provides a bright potential for the revolutionary advance.

The Cerezo administration is gradually isolating itself from private enterprise, the Church, and the unions. The most important conflict is now occurring between the Christian Democratic government and the army.

The Cerezo policy from the very beginning tried to weaken the military apparatus, not to eliminate it as an instrument of power, but to put it under his control for the service of his party. Toward this end he proceeded to cut the defense budget, to neglect military aid from imperialism, to eliminate supply sources from Israel and Taiwan, and to threaten investigation of the massacres and disappearances carried out by the military.

According to our intelligence sources, at this moment there is a high degree of confrontation, and it is believed that a coup d'état is very near. Under current circumstances, this event will not benefit the Revolution, since the contradictions are not yet at the proper level. We should support Cerezo to carry out his program, which in the end will separate even more the sectors that sustain the wealthy middle class, and will cripple the army as final bastion of the reactionaries. The final result will allow an increased operational field to reach our objectives, regrouping forces and initiating the offensive.

In the event that a military coup occurs, we will sponsor the marriage between the resented and out-of-power Christian Democrats with the revolutionary groups, which will renew the class struggle and will totally divide the society.

b. El Salvador

We cannot allow under any circumstances, based upon the Esquipulas II treaty, the retreat of revolutionary Salvadoran organizations; on the contrary, the level of military confrontations should be maintained and increased. It will be advisable, however, to incorporate our political schemes into the civil struggle by taking advantage of political space the agreements have opened. Using the amnesty, Comrades Ungo and Zamora dialogues, and organizational efforts, some of the combatants should incorporate into the unions, Church, associations, and other groups so they can do political work, be used as a catalyst, and echo the armed struggle. We will then be rebuilding the two dimensions of the war and liberation; the political area and the military area. This movement is of key importance in order to advantageously reestablish the revolutionary struggle.

c. Panama

It is obvious that, in order to remove the attention from Nicaragua, and from the potential anti-imperialist character that this conflict implies, we should support Noriega. Our support to Noriega should be done very carefully, owing to his middle-class weakness and his delinquent and corrupt mentality, since he probably will not be able to endure the imperialist pressures, forcing him to resign sooner or later.

An additional advantage is that the increased contradictions that are occurring in the Panamanian situation will polarize the society, allowing, in the medium term, the advance of the revolutionary struggle.

Rather than support Noriega, our support will be to our revolutionary comrades within the PRD.

d. Costa Rica

In Costa Rica, Oscar Arias has shown pragmatism by accepting the Sandinista Popular Revolution.

At this moment, by winning the Nobel Prize, he will be more prudent when appraising the Revolution, and will not take drastic attitudes that are not in accordance with the prize.

Our policy should be oriented to consolidate his leadership within the Partido de Liberación Nacional, so it can be projected beyond his presidential mandate.

The personal vanity of Arias is our best ally, and we will cultivate it in order to reach our goals.

We will continue at the same time providing support and military training to the Costa Rican revolutionaries, so will have our options open, and will encourage the careful infiltration of our comrades in the Party's structure of Liberación Nacional. Based on this framework we will oppose any premature action from any group that is aimed to overthrow the government.

e. Honduras

Our policy toward the puppet government of Honduras must be prudent, knowing that it is the bait placed by imperialism; it does not mean that we should remain idle.

First we will induce the rejection of the masses and their

organizers with the presence of the counterrevolution. Simultaneously, we will encourage nationalism against the presence of North American military bases.

Second, we will totally support the revolutionary organizations in their search for a symmetry between them and the counterrevolution.

Finally, our strategy objectives are to consolidate the Sandinista Popular Revolution in Nicaragua, and to drive the development of contradictions in Central America, so the advance of the anti-imperialist revolutionary struggle is facilitated. FREE COUNTRY OR DEATH!

Notes

INTRODUCTION

1. David Rees, *The Age of Containment: The Cold War 1945–1965* (London: Macmillan and Co., Ltd., 1967), pp. 24–25. See also Howard Trivers, *Lectures on Foreign Affairs* (Muncie: Ball State University, 1974), p. 17. Numerous writers date the onset of World War III from this time (1944–1947), including such authors as James Burnham, Sir Robert Thompson, Alexander Solzhenitsyn, Jillian Becker, and Brian Crozier. See especially the latter's "Security and the Myth of 'Peace': Surviving the Third World War," *Conflict Studies*, no. 76 (October 1976), pp. 1–4.

2. U.S. Congress, Senate Committee on the Judiciary, *Hearings Before the Subcommittee to Investigate the Administration of the Internal Security Act*, 86th Cong., 2nd sess., part 8A, memorandum 11, May 9, 1960, p. 531. Cited hereinafter as Eastland-Dodd *Hearings*.

3. Cecil B. Lyon, "Bogotá, April 9," *American Foreign Service Journal* 25, no. 5 (May 1948), p. 7.

4. Eastland-Dodd *Hearings*, part 10, testimony of William D. Pawley, September 2 and 8, 1960, p. 725.

5. Forrest C. Pogue, *George C. Marshall: Statesman, 1945–1959* (New York: Viking, 1987), p. 393.

6. Josef Kalvoda, "Communist Strategy in Latin America," *Yale Review* LV (Winter 1965), p. 196.

7. U.S. Congress, Senate Committee on the Judiciary, *Hearings Before the Subcommittee to Investigate the Administration of the Internal Security Act* (International Terrorism), 94th Cong., 1st sess., part 4, testimony of Brian Crozier, May 14, 1975, p. 184. See also Josef Kalvoda, "Communist Strategy in Latin America," *Yale Review* L (Autumn 1960), pp. 37–41.

8. Paul D. Bethel, *The Losers: The Definitive Report, by an Eye Witness, of the Communist Conquest of Cuba and the Soviet Penetration in Latin America* (New Rochelle, N.Y.: Arlington House, 1969), pp. 22–24.

9. Carlos Rangel, *The Latin Americans: Their Love-Hate Relationship with the United States*, rev. ed. (New Brunswick, N.J.: Transaction Books, 1987), p. 52. See also D. Bruce Jackson, *Castro, The Kremlin, and Communism in Latin America* (Baltimore: Johns Hopkins Press, 1969), p. 156, fn. 1.

10. Author's interview with Dr. Oscar Sevilla Sacasa, July 19, 1988. See also *Foreign Relations of the United States, 1955–1957, American Republics*, vol. 6, Memorandum of a Conversation, December 6, 1956 (Washington, D.C.: U.S. Government Printing Office, 1987), p. 838.

11. Norman A. Charité, et al., *Case Study in Insurgency and Revolutionary Warfare: Guatemala 1944–1954*, Special Operations Research Office (Washington, D.C.: American University, 1964), p. 87.

12. Eastland-Dodd *Hearings*, part 13, testimony of Andrés Pérez-Chaumont, March 29, 1961, pp. 832–33.

13. Eastland-Dodd *Hearings*, part 1, testimony of Major Pedro L. Díaz Lanz, July 14, 1959, pp. 15–16. See also part 7, testimony of Colonel Manuel Antonio Ugalde Carrillo, May 1960, pp. 399–401.

14. The issue of clandestine military support of the Sandinistas is examined in the following chapter, but a useful article on it is

by Constantine Menges, "Central America and Its Enemies," *Commentary* 72, no. 2 (August 1981), pp. 32–38.

15. Juan Vives, *Los amos de Cuba* (Buenos Aires: Emece Editores S.A., 1982), p. 79.

16. Mikhail Heller and Aleksandr M. Nekrich, *Utopia in Power: The History of the Soviet Union from 1917 to the Present* (New York: Summit Books, 1982–86), p. 503.

17. Charité, et al., *Insurgency and Warfare*, pp. 82–83, 88–91.

18. Eastland-Dodd *Hearings*, part 16, testimony of Paul D. Bethel, March 7, 1967, p. 1093. See also *The Tricontinental Conference of African, Asian, and Latin American Peoples*, prepared for the Subcommittee to Investigate the Administration of the Internal Security Act, Committee on the Judiciary, U.S. Senate Staff Study, 89th Congress, 2nd sess. (Washington, D.C.: U.S. Government Printing Office, 1966), pp. 1–4.

19. Fayne Monahan, "The Soviet Union and the Global Chess Game" (seminar paper, Webster University, Spring 1988), p. 6. See also Edgar O'Ballance, *Tracks of the Bear* (Novato, Calif.: Presidio Press, 1982), p. 174.

20. Stetson Conn and Byron Fairchild, *The Framework of Hemispheric Defense, The Western Hemisphere: U.S. Army in World War II* (Washington, D.C.: Office of the Chief of Military History, Department of the Army, 1960), p. 418.

21. See Lewis A. Tambs, "Estrátegic, poder naval e sobrevivéncia: argumentos para manter o canal do Panamá," *A Defesa Nacional* (Rio de Janeiro) 66, 682 (1979), pp. 105–115.

22. Lewis A. Tambs, "The Influence of Geopolitics in the Formulation of International Policy and the Strategy of Great Powers," International Symposium on International Policy and Strategy (São Paulo, 1979), pp. 35–36. This symposium paper was published the following year. See "A Influencia da Geopolitica na Politica e na Estrátegia das Grandes Potencias," *A Defesa Nacional* (Rio de Janeiro) 67, 690 (1980), pp. 127–156.

23. Cole Blasier, *The Giant's Rival: The USSR and Latin America*, rev. ed. (Pittsburgh: University of Pittsburgh, 1987), p. 227, fn. 19.

CHAPTER 1

1. For a brief discussion of this strategy, see U.S. Congress, Senate Committee on the Judiciary, *Hearings Before the Subcommittee on Security and Terrorism* (Historical Antecedents of Soviet Terrorism), 97th Cong., 1st sess., June 12, 1981, p. 71. See also Daniel James, *Cuba: The First Soviet Satellite in the Americas* (New York: Avon, 1961), pp. 83–84.

2. Paul D. Bethel, *The Losers* (New Rochelle, N.Y.: Arlington House, 1969), p. 72.

3. Charles E. Bohlen, *Witness to History, 1929–1969* (New York: W. W. Norton and Co., 1973), p. 496.

4. Mario Lazo, *Dagger in the Heart: American Policy Failures in Cuba* (New York: Twin Circle Publishing Co., 1968), p. 255.

5. Brian Crozier, "The Satellization of Cuba," *Conflict Studies*, no. 35 (1973), p. 5. See also Samuel T. Francis, *The Soviet Strategy of Terror* (Washington, D.C.: Heritage Foundation, 1981), p. 7.

6. Bethel, *The Losers*, p. 121.

7. Georgie Ann Geyer, "Los sandinistas nunca escondieron lo que eran," *Diario las Americas*, January 5, 1988, p. 4A. Geyer's article is based on her interview with Fausto Amador, brother of the late Carlos Fonseca, the first Sandinista and the first trained in Moscow. See also, Humberto Belli, "Three Nicaraguans on the Betrayal of Their Revolution," *The Heritage Lectures*, no. 41 (Washington, D.C.: Heritage Foundation, 1985), p. 4.

8. Lawrence E. Harrison, as director of the United States AID mission to Managua between 1979 and 1981, tried courageously to establish friendly relations with the new Nicaraguan government. See his article "Rebuffed by the Sandinistas," *Boston Globe*, July 19, 1983, p. 11.

9. Lazo, *Dagger in the Heart*, pp. 224–26.

10. Cleto Di Giovanni, Jr., and M. L. Harvey, *Crisis in Central America: Facts, Arguments, Importance, Dangers, Ramifications*

(Coral Gables, Fla.: Advanced International Studies Institute, University of Miami, 1982), p. 43.

11. Bethel, *The Losers*, p. 52.

12. R. A. Hudson, "Castro's America Department: Systemizing Insurgencies in Latin America," *Terrorism: An International Journal* 9, no. 2 (1987), pp. 131–33.

13. Francis, *Soviet Strategy of Terror*, p. 9.

14. U.S. Congress, House of Representatives Subcommittee on Inter-American Affairs, Committee on Foreign Affairs, *Castro Communist Subversion in the Western Hemisphere*, House Report 195 (1963), p. 430.

15. Spruille Braden, *Diplomats and Demagogues: The Memoirs of Spruille Braden* (New Rochelle, N.Y.: Arlington House, 1971), p. 430; also Paul D. Bethel, "The Havana Conference," *The Reporter*, March 24, 1966, pp. 25–26.

16. U.S. Congress, Senate Staff Study, *The Tricontinental Conference of African, Asian, and Latin American Peoples*, prepared for the Subcommittee to Investigate the Internal Security Act, 89th Cong., 2nd sess. (1966), pp. 33–35.

17. Bethel, *The Losers*, pp. 13–14.

18. Antonio J. Ybarra-Rojas, "The Cuban-Nicaraguan Connection," in *Cuban Communism*, 6th ed., Irving Louis Horowitz, ed. (New Brunswick, N.J.: Transactions Books, 1987), pp. 69–71. See also Shirley Christian, *Nicaragua: Revolution in the Family* (New York: Vintage Books, 1986), pp. 32–33.

19. Author's interview with Dr. Oscar Sevilla Sacasa, July 19, 1988. See also Douglas W. Payne, "The 'Mantos' of Sandinista Deception," *Strategic Review* (Spring 1985), pp. 9–12.

20. U.S. Congress, Senate Committee on the Judiciary, *Hearings before the Subcommittee to Investigate the Administration of the Internal Security Act*, 86th Cong., 2nd sess., part 20, testimony of Orlando Castro Hidalgo, October 16, 1969, p. 1449.

21. Crozier, "Satellization of Cuba," p. 14. See also Timothy Ashby, *The Bear in the Back Yard: Moscow's Caribbean Strategy* (Lexington, Mass.: Lexington Books, 1987), p. 50.

22. Senate *Hearings on Security and Terrorism*, 2nd sess. (Role

of Cuba in International Terrorism and Subversion), testimony of Gerardo Peraza, February 26, 1982, p. 9.

23. Hudson, "Castro's America Department," p. 134. See also Francis, *Soviet Strategy of Terror* (1985 ed.), pp. 3–4.

24. David Nolan, *The Ideology of the Sandinistas and the Nicaraguan Revolution* (Coral Gables, Fla.: Institute of Interamerican Studies, Graduate School of International Studies, 1984), pp. 36–37.

25. Humberto Belli, *Breaking Faith: The Sandinista Revolution*, Puebla Institute (Westchester, Ill.: Crossway Books, 1985), pp. 15–16.

26. U.S. Department of State, *Cuba's Renewed Support for Violence in Latin America*, Special Report 90, Bureau of Public Affairs (Washington, D.C.: Government Printing Office, 1981), pp. 5–6.

27. Ashby, *Bear in the Back Yard*, p. 103.

28. Francis, *Soviet Strategy of Terror* (1985 ed.), pp. 64–66. See also Giovanni and Harvey, *Crisis in Central America*, pp. 47–48.

29. Hudson, "Castro's America Department," pp. 128–30.

30. Peter Babej, "Soviet Strategy in Nicaragua: The Military Dimension" (Seminar paper, Harvard University, January 29, 1988), appendix I, p. xii, fn. 29.

31. Mikhail Heller and Aleksandr M. Nekrich, *Utopia in Power: The History of the Soviet Union from 1917 to the Present* (New York: Summit Books, 1982–86), p. 704. See also Arkady N. Shevchenko, *Breaking With Moscow* (New York: Alfred A. Knopf, 1985), pp. 235–37.

32. Shevchenko, *Breaking With Moscow*, p. 183.

33. Heller and Nekrich, *Utopia in Power*, pp. 647–48. See also Wolfgang Leonhard, *The Kremlin and the West: A Realist Approach* (New York: W.W. Norton and Co., 1984), pp. 132–34.

34. Robert A. Ford, "The Soviet Union: The Next Decade," *Foreign Affairs* 62 (Summer 1984), p. 1141.

35. See, e.g., John Norton Moore and Robert F. Turner, *Inter-*

national Law and the Brezhnev Doctrine (Lanham, Md.: University Press of America, 1987), p. 118.

36. Pamela S. Falk, *Cuban Foreign Policy* (Lexington, Mass.: Lexington Books, 1986), appendix 1, p. 240.

37. Report to the Committee on International Relations, U.S. House of Representatives, Senior Specialists Division, Congressional Research Series, Library of Congress, *The Soviet Union and the Third World: A Watershed in Great Power Policy?*, 95th Cong., 1st sess., May 1977, p. 144.

38. Report prepared for the Subcommittee on Security and Terrorism, Committee on the Judiciary, U.S. Senate, *State-Sponsored Terrorism*, 99th Cong., 1st sess., June 1985, pp. 11, 88–89.

CHAPTER 2

1. David Nolan, *The Ideology of the Sandinistas and the Nicaraguan Revolution* (Coral Gables, Fla.: Institute of Interamerican Studies, University of Miami, 1984), p. 60.

2. *Ally Betrayed . . . Nicaragua* (Alexandria, Va.: Western Goals, 1980); Postscript by former U.S. Ambassador to Nicaragua, Turner B. Shelton, pp. 69–70.

3. Mikhail Gorbachev, *Perestroika: New Thinking for Our Country and the World* (New York: Harper and Row, 1987), p. 175.

4. Timothy Ashby, *The Bear in the Back Yard: Moscow's Caribbean Strategy* (Lexington, Mass.: Lexington Books, 1987), pp. 103–04. See also Roger Fontaine, "Cuba's Terrorist Connection," *Backgrounder*, June 4, 1988, p. 11.

5. *Ally Betrayed*, appendix IV, p. 94.

6. U.S. Department of State, *Cuba's Renewed Support for Violence in Latin America*, Special Report 90 (Washington, D.C.: Government Printing Office, 1981), p. 6.

7. U.S. Congress, House of Representatives Committee on Merchant Marine and Fisheries, *Hearings Before the Subcommittee on the Panama Canal* (Panama Gunrunning), 96th Cong., 1st

sess., testimony of Lieut. General Gordon Sumner, Jr., June 7, 1979, pp. 122–23.

8. Daniel James, "Moscow's Friend?" *Orbis: A Journal of World Affairs* 33 (Winter 1988), p. 66.

9. Ibid., p. 67.

10. House of Representatives *Hearings on Panama Canal*, statement by Luis Pallais, June 6, 1979, p. 58.

11. Uri Ra'anam, et al., *Hydra of Carnage: The International Linkages of Terrorism and Other Low-Intensity Operations; The Witnesses Speak* (Lexington, Mass.: Lexington Books, 1986), appendix A, p. 302.

12. *Analysis of the Situation and Tasks of the Sandinista People's Revolution; Political and Military Theses Presented by the National Directorate of the Sandinista National Liberation Front at the Assembly of Cadres*, September 21–23, 1979. (Originally published in Spanish in October 1979; often referred to as the "72-Hour Document.")

13. U.S. Department of State, *The "72-Hour Document"; The Sandinista Blueprint for Constructing Communism in Nicaragua*, Coordinator of Public Diplomacy for Latin America and the Caribbean (Washington, D.C.: Government Printing Office, 1986). The earliest references to this important document in English did not appear until 1985. See, e.g., Shirley Christian, *Nicaragua: Revolution in the Family* (1985), Humberto Belli, *Breaking Faith* (1985), and Douglas W. Payne, *The Democratic Mask: The Consolidation of the Sandinista Revolution* (1985).

14. Lawrence E. Harrison, "The Confrontation with the Sandinistas: Myths and Realities," *Public Law Review* 6, no. 1 (1987), p. 36.

15. Herbert Romerstein, *Soviet Support for International Terrorism* (Washington, D.C.: Foundation for Democratic Education, 1981), pp. 17–18.

16. Ashby, *Bear in the Back Yard*, p. 107.

17. Ra'anam, *Hydra of Carnage* (testimony of Miguel Bolaños Hunter), pp. 318–19.

18. Ashby, *Bear in the Back Yard*, p. 113.

19. Georges Fauriol, ed., *Latin American Insurgencies* (Washington, D.C.: National Defense University Press, 1985), p. 47.

20. Y. V. Andropov, *Speeches and Writings* (Oxford: Pergamon Press, 1983), p. 31.

21. Ra'anam, *Hydra of Carnage* (testimony of Bolaños Hunter), p. 312.

22. U.S. Congress, Senate Committee on the Judiciary, *Hearings Before the Subcommittee on Security and Terrorism* (Terrorism: The Role of Moscow and Its Subcontractors), 97th Cong., 1st sess., June 1981, p. 49. Robert Moss, who testified in this regard, later used that information as the basis for his novel *Monimbó*. See Robert Moss and A. de Borchgrave, *Monimbó* (New York: Simon and Schuster, 1983), pp. 5–10.

23. U.S. Department of State, *Nicaragua's Interior Ministry: Instrument of Political Consolidation*, Bureau of Inter-American Affairs (Washington, D.C.: Government Printing Office, 1987), pp. 2–3.

24. Ibid., p. 3.

25. U.S. Department of State, *Inside the Sandinista Regime: A Special Investigator's Perspective*, Bureau of Inter-American Affairs (Washington, D.C.: Government Printing Office, 1987), p. 13.

26. *Encuesta de opinión: Análisis de métodos, resultados y conclusiones* (Managua: INEC, 1981). See also *El Nuevo Diario* (Managua), January 28, 1982, p. 4.

27. U.S. Department of State, *Nicaragua's Interior Ministry*, p. 11. The national election held in Nicaragua in 1984 has been analyzed and exhaustively documented by Alejandro Bolaños G. in *1984 in Managua: The 1984 Sandinista elections; Nicaraguan Research Project Occasional Paper* (Coral Gables, Fla.: Institute of Interamerican Studies, University of Miami, August 1988), pp. 1–8.

28. See, e.g., the U.S. Department of State publication *Attack on the Church: Persecution of the Catholic Church in Nicaragua* (July 1986), 21pp. Even an editorial in the *New York Times* on July 10, 1986, referring to the FSLN's seven-year war to destroy

Nicaragua's Catholic Church, concluded that the democratic revolution against Somoza has been "hopelessly betrayed."

29. Xavier Zavala, "Status of Education in Nicaragua," *Voices Against the State: Nicaraguan Opposition to the FSLN; The Nicaraguan Research Project*, Steven Blakemore, ed. (Coral Gables, Fla.: Institute of Interamerican Studies, University of Miami, 1988), pp. 1–4.

30. Humberto Belli, "A Martial Plan for Central America," *Policy Review*, no. 44 (Spring 1988), p. 66.

31. Zavala, "Status of Education in Nicaragua," p. 11.

32. Mikhail Heller, *Cogs in the Wheel: The Formation of Soviet Man* (New York: Alfred A. Knopf, 1988), pp. 31–41.

CHAPTER 3

1. John Norton Moore, "The Secret War in Central America and the Future of World Order," *American Journal of International Law* 80, no. 1 (January 1986), pp. 44–45.

2. U.S. Congress, House of Representatives Committee on Merchant Marine and Fisheries, *Hearings Before the Subcommittee on the Panama Canal* (Panama Gunrunning), 96th Cong., 1st sess.; statement by Lieut. General Gordon Sumner, Jr., June 7, 1979, p.125.

3. U.S. Congress, House of Representatives, *Hearing Before the Committee on Foreign Affairs* (Nicaraguan Government Involvement in Narcotics Trafficking), 99th Cong., 2nd sess.; statement by Alvaro José Baldizón Avilés, March 11, 1986, p. 38.

4. *Nicaragua, Civil Liberties, and the Central American Peace Plan* (New York: Puebla Institute, 1988), p. 78.

5. U.S. Department of State, *Human Rights Under the Sandinistas: From Revolution to Repression*, no. 9467 (Washington, D.C.: Government Printing Office, 1986), p. 219.

6. Moore, "The Secret War in Central America," p. 46.

7. U.S. Department of State, *Nicaragua's Interior Ministry: Instrument of Political Consolidation*, Bureau of Inter-American

Affairs (Washington, D.C.: Government Printing Office, 1987), p. 6.

8. U.S. Department of State, *Sandinista Prisons: A Tool of Intimidation*, Bureau of Inter-American Affairs (Washington, D.C.: Government Printing Office, 1986), p. 3.

9. *Nicaragua, Civil Liberties, and the Central American Peace Plan*, pp. 20–21. See also Douglas W. Payne, "Human Rights in Nicaragua," *Public Law Review* 6, no. 1 (1987), pp. 54–55.

10. U.S. Department of State, *Broken Promises: Sandinista Repression of Human Rights in Nicaragua*, Office of Public Diplomacy for Latin America and the Caribbean (Washington, D.C.: Government Printing Office, 1984), pp. 7–22. See also Jack Cox, *Requiem in the Tropics; Inside Central America* (Evanston, Ill.: UCA Books, 1987), pp. 108–120.

11. Nina H. Shea, "Testimony for Nicaraguan Refugees," *Nicaragua in Focus* 1, no. 4 (1987), p. 19.

12. John Norton Moore, "Legal Issues in the Central American Conflict," Remarks before the annual meeting of the American Society for International Law, April 25, 1985, p. 3.

13. Martin Kriele, *Nicaragua—America's Bleeding Heart* (Mainz, West Germany: V. Hase & Koehler Verlag, 1985/86), pp. 38, 72–73.

14. U.S. Congress, House Committee on Foreign Affairs, *Hearings Before the Subcommittee on Inter-American Affairs*, 96th Cong., 2nd sess.; statement by Congressman C. W. (Bill) Young, September 30, 1980, p. 16.

15. Department of State, *Sandinista Prisons*, report by Wesley Smith, p. 3.

16. Esquipulas had been the site of an earlier (May 1986) meeting of the five Central American presidents, although no agreement had been reached.

17. Dirección Nacional FSLN, Borrador, Protocolo 1740, Sesión Extraordinaria No. 47, "Estrategia 1988," p. 2. See Appendix 2.

18. Lars Schoultz, *National Security and United States Policy*

Toward Latin America (Princeton: Princeton University Press, 1987), pp. 227–29.

19. Letter from Dr. Alejandro Bolaños Geyer to the author, March 23, 1986.

20. Ronald Reagan, "Address Before a Joint Session of the Congress on Central America," April 27, 1983, *Public Papers of the Presidents of the United States* (Washington, D.C.: Government Printing Office, 1984), p. 605.

21. U.S. General Accounting Office, *Immigration: Studies of the Immigration and Control Act's Impact on Mexico* (Washington, D.C.: Government Printing Office, 1988), p. 2.

22. *Fleeing Their Homeland: A Report on the Testimony of Nicaraguan Refugees to Conditions in Their Country and the Reasons for Their Flight* (New York: Puebla Institute, 1987), pp. 3, 13.

23. Shea, "Testimony for Nicaraguan Refugees," pp. 18–19.

24. *Fleeing Their Homeland*, pp. 3–10.

25. Milton H. Jamail and Chandler Stolp, "Central Americans on the Run: Political Refugees or Economic Migrants?" *Public Affairs Comment* 31, no. 3 (Spring 1985), p. 1.

26. Jamail and Stolp, "Central Americans on the Run," pp. 1–2.

27. *Fleeing Their Homeland*, pp. 18–19.

28. U.S. General Accounting Office, *Report to the Congress of the United States; Central American Refugees: Regional Conditions and Prospects and Potential Impact on the United States* (Washington, D.C.: Government Printing Office, 1984), p. IV.

29. *St. Louis Post-Dispatch*, December 26, 1988, p. 8A.

CHAPTER 4

1. U.S. Department of State, "Soviet Bloc Assistance to Cuba and Nicaragua," *Latin America Dispatch* (October 1987), p. 1. See also Robert F. Turner, *Nicaragua v. United States: A Look at the Facts, Special Report 1987* (Washington, D.C.: Pergamon-Brassey's International Defense Pub., 1987), pp. 2–3.

2. Arturo Cruz Sequeira, "The Origins of Sandinista Foreign

Policy," in *Central America: Anatomy of Conflict*, Robert S. Leiken, ed. (New York: Pergamon Press, 1984), p. 104.

3. Lawrence E. Harrison, "We Tried to Accept Nicaragua's Revolution," *Washington Post*, June 30, 1983; and "Sandinists' 'Foreign Devil,'" *New York Times*, March 3, 1982. See also Harrison's more recent article in the *Washington Post*, March 31, 1988, p. 23A.

4. U.S. Department of State and the Department of Defense, *The Sandinista Military Build-up*, Inter-American Series, 199 (May 1985), p. 35.

5. U.S. Department of State, *Broken Promises: Sandinista Repression of Human Rights in Nicaragua*, Office of Public Diplomacy for Latin America and the Caribbean (Washington, D.C.: Government Printing Office, 1984), p. 7.

6. U.S. Department of State, *Broken Promises*, p. 6.

7. U.S. Departments of State and Defense, *The Sandinista Military Build-up*, p. 7.

8. Transcript of interview on October 1, 1987 (name withheld).

9. U.S. Departments of State and Defense, *The Sandinista Military Build-up*, pp. 11–12.

10. *For your Eyes Only: An Open Intelligence Summary of Current Military Affairs* 182, February 15, 1988 (Amarillo, Tex.: Tiger Pub., P.O. Box 8759, 79114), p. 3.

11. U.S. Departments of State and Defense, *The Sandinista Military Build-up*, p. 4.

12. U.S. Department of State and the Department of Defense, *Background Paper: Nicaragua's Military Build-up and Support for Central American Subversion* (July 18, 1984), p. 17.

13. U.S. Departments of State and Defense, *Background Paper*, pp. 9–10.

14. Off-loaded from the Soviet ship *Bakuriani*, delivery of the first MI-24 HIND-Ds coincided with the U.S. presidential election of November 1984. See Mary Desjeans and Peter Clement's "Soviet Policy Toward Central America," *Proceedings of the Academy of Political Science* 36, no. 4 (1987), p. 225.

15. Peter Babej, "Soviet Strategy in Nicaragua: The Military Dimension" (Seminar paper, Harvard University, January 29, 1988), p. 32.

16. U.S. Departments of State and Defense, *The Sandinista Military Build-up*, p. 17.

17. U.S. Department of State and Department of Defense, *The Soviet-Cuban Connection in Central America and the Caribbean* (April 1985), p. 27.

18. U.S. Departments of State and Defense, *Background Paper*, pp. 10–11.

19. "Nicaragua May Increase Forces to 600,000," *St. Louis Post-Dispatch*, December 13, 1987, p. 5A.

20. See, e.g., Stephen Kinzer's article in the *New York Times*, December 14, 1987.

21. "Revelaciones de un ex-sandinista," *Selecciones del Reader's Digest* (July 1988), p. 55.

22. Transcript of interview held on April 8–9, 1988 (name withheld). But see U.S. Department of State Special Report 132, *"Revolution Beyond our Borders"; Sandinista Intervention in Central America* (September 1985).

23. U.S. Congress, Senate Committee on the Judiciary, Report prepared for the Subcommittee on Security and Terrorism, *State-Sponsored Terrorism*, 99th Cong., 1st sess., June 1985 (Washington, D.C.: Government Printing Office, 1985), p. 23, fn. 1.

24. "Cuba's Terrorist Connection," *Backgrounder* (June 4, 1988), p. 10.

25. U.S. Congress, Senate Committee on the Judiciary, *Hearings Before the Subcommittee to Investigate the Internal Security Act* (International Terrorism), 94th Cong., 1st sess., part 4, May 14, 1975, pp. 184–85.

26. R. A. Hudson, "Castro's America Department: Systemizing Insurgencies in Latin America," *Terrorism: An International Journal* 9, no. 2 (1987), p. 128.

27. Jiri Valenta, "The USSR, Cuba, and the Crisis in Central America," *Orbis: A Journal of World Affairs* 25, n. 3 (Fall 1981), p. 734.

28. U.S. Congress, House of Representatives, *Hearings Before the Subcommittee on Foreign Affairs* (Review of the Presidential Certification of Nicaragua's Connection to Terrorism), 96th Cong., 2nd sess., September 30, 1980, p. 27.

29. Diplomatically, the Nandaime incident was serious since it resulted in the unnecessary expulsion of the U.S. ambassador to Nicaragua and seven other U.S. Embassy personnel. The United States swiftly retaliated in kind by withdrawing the visas of the Nicaraguan ambassador to Washington and seven other diplomatic personnel, including, as it turned out, Nicaragua's military representative on the Inter-American Defense Board in Washington.

30. Peter Clement, "Moscow and Nicaragua: Two Sides of Soviet Policy," *Comparative Strategy: An International Journal* 5, no. 1 (1985), p. 79.

31. Peter Clement, "The USSR and the Nicaraguan Revolution: The Superpower Dimension," paper prepared for the 19th annual meeting of the American Association for the Advancement of Slavic Studies, November 1987), p. 18.

32. U.S. Departments of State and Defense, *Background Paper*, pp. 15–19.

33. Uri Ra'anam, et al., *Hydra of Carnage: The International Linkages of Terrorism and Other Low-Intensity Operations; The Witnesses Speak* (Lexington, MA: Lexington Books, 1986), appendix A, p. 318.

CHAPTER 5

1. Mikhail Heller, *Cogs in the Wheel: The Formation of Soviet Man* (New York: Alfred A. Knopf, 1988), pp. 4–6, 20–27. On the "human cost" of communism before 1959, see, e.g., Alexander Solzhenitsyn, *Warning to the West* (New York: Farrar, Straus and Giroux, 1975–76), pp. 128–29.

2. Constantine C. Menges, "The Record of the United States and the Soviet Union in Post-World War II International Politics," in *Arms Control: The American Dilemma*, William R. Kintner, ed. (Washington, D.C.: Washington Institute, 1987), pp. 11–36.

3. Lewis A. Tambs, "Socializing the Soviets; Or How to Lose World War III," *Saturday Magazine*, December 29, 1979, p. 2.

4. Tambs, "Socializing the Soviets," pp. 2–4.

5. Arkady N. Shevchenko, *Breaking with Moscow* (New York: Alfred A. Knopf, 1985), p. 368. But see the original source of this quotation in Richard Pipes, "Can the Soviet Union Reform?" *Foreign Affairs* 63 (Fall 1984), p. 59.

6. Christopher Felix (pseudonym), *A Short Course in the Secret War* (New York: E. P. Dutton and Co., 1963), p. 23.

7. Josef Kalvoda, "Communist Strategy in Latin America," *Yale Review* 55, no. 2 (Winter 1965), pp. 191–95; Felix, *A Short Course in the Secret War*, pp. 23–24.

8. U.S. Department of State, *Guatemala: A Case History of Communist Penetration*, Inter-American Series 52 (1957), pp. 66–69.

9. Lewis A. Tambs, "La década roja de Guatemala, 1944–1954," *Problemas del Comunismo* 11 (Sept.–Oct. 1964), p. 70.

10. Doubtless, Castro advised the Sandinistas not to follow his lead by severing ties with the United States.

11. Bill Gertz, "'62 Cuban Crisis Viewed by Analysts as Tendering Hemisphere to Soviets," *Washington Times*, October 22, 1987.

12. Lewis A. Tambs, "Righting the Dominoes: Democracy, Self-Determination, and Ideological Dictators," *New World: A Journal of Latin American Studies* 2 (1987), p. 3.

13. Samuel T. Francis, *The Soviet Strategy of Terror* (Washington, D.C.: Heritage Foundation, 1985), p. 80.

14. The U.S. principle of national self-defense lies at the core of the Monroe Doctrine itself, and was invoked in both World War I and World War II. In 1917, President Wilson invoked it in purchasing the Danish West Indies, and in August 1940, President Roosevelt invoked the principle in response to Prime Minister Churchill's request for fifty American destroyers. See, respectively, Albert K. Weinberg, *Manifest Destiny: A Study of Nationalist Expansionism in American History* (Baltimore: Johns Hopkins Press, 1935), p. 382; and Warren F. Kimball, ed., *Chur-*

chill & Roosevelt: The Complete Correspondence, Vol. I, 1933–1942 (Princeton: Princeton University Press, 1984), p. 59.

15. Tambs, "Righting the Dominoes," p. 2.

16. From transcript of conversation with Professor Wolfgang Leonhard, January 26, 1989.

17. From transcript of conversations with Stanislav Levchenko, December 13, 1988, and with Wolfgang Leonhard. On the food crisis in the USSR, see, e.g., David Remmick's article in the *Washington Post*, August 28, 1988, p. A31.

18. Shevchenko, *Breaking with Moscow*, p. 367.

19. Dirección Nacional FSLN, Borrador Protocolo 1740, Sesión Extraordinaria No. 47, "Estrategia 1988," pp. 1–2.

20. Wolfgang Leonhard, *The Kremlin and the West: A Realistic Approach* (New York: W. W. Norton and Co., 1984), p. 153.

21. Austria was thereby neutralized, thus affecting NATO's supply lines.

22. Wolfgang Leonhard, "Soviet Foreign Policy: Interests, Motives and Objectives" (paper, May 1983), pp. 15–16. A version of this paper was subsequently published in *Soviet Politics in the Eighties*, Helmut Sonnenfeldt, ed. (Boulder: Westview Press, 1984).

23. Leonhard, "Soviet Foreign Policy," pp. 16–17.

24. Mikhail Voslenski, *Nomenklatura: The Soviet Ruling Class* (New York: Doubleday & Co., 1984), pp. 326–27.

25. Leonhard, "Soviet Foreign Policy," p. 12. See also Tambs, "Socializing the Soviets," pp. 2–4, and Voslenski, "The Claim to World Hegemony" in *Nomenklatura*, pp. 319–354.

26. Richard Pipes, "Soviet Global Strategy," *Commentary* 69, no. 4 (April 1980), p. 39.

27. Dirección Nacional FSLN, "Estrategia 1988," pp. 6–10. See, in this regard, the testimony of former U.N. Ambassador Jeane Kirkpatrick before the Senate Armed Services Committee on January 28, 1986; U.S. Congress, Senate, *Hearing Before the Committee on Armed Services* (State-Sponsored Terrorism), 99th Cong., 2nd sess., pp. 8–10.

CHAPTER 6

1. Doubtless, readers interested in this crucial issue and others related thereto will benefit from reading an insider's account during these pivotal years of the Reagan administration. See, in this regard, Constantine C. Menges, *Inside the National Security Council: The True Story of the Making and Unmaking of Reagan's Foreign Policy* (New York: Simon and Schuster, 1988), pp. 93–96, 103–9; *passim.*

2. Susan Kaufman Purcell, "The Choice in Central America," *Foreign Affairs* 66 (Fall 1987), p. 119. Purcell also cites "Soviet bloc" aid to the Sandinistas, between 1979 and 1983, as totaling $3 billion.

3. Interview with Dr. Oscar Sevilla Sacasa, July 19, 1988.

4. Timothy Ashby, *The Bear in the Back Yard: Moscow's Caribbean Strategy* (Lexington, Mass.: Lexington Books, 1987), p. 183.

5. U.S. Department of State, *Guatemala: A Case History of Communist Penetration*, Inter-American Series 52 (1957), p. 67. "Due to the fact that the concerns of our strategic ally, the Soviet Union, are mainly concentrated on the geopolitical problems . . . we should expect that their military aid will continue to arrive according to our needs, *but we should not expect the same on the economic assistance that we need so urgently.*" (Italics added.) See Chapter 5, fn. 19.

6. Ronald Reagan, "Address Before a Joint Session of the Congress on the State of the Union," February 6, 1985, *Public Papers of the Presidents of the United States, 1985* (Washington, D.C.: Government Printing Office, 1988), p. 135.

7. Howard J. Wiarda, "Updating U.S. Strategic Policy: Containment in the Caribbean Basin," in *Containment: Concept and Policy, Vol. II*, Terry L. Deibel and John Lewis Gaddis, eds. (Washington, D.C.: National Defense University Press, 1986), pp. 559–60.

8. Lewis A. Tambs, "The Future Belongs to the Free—The

Reagan Doctrine and Central America," *Vital Speeches of the Day* 12 (April 1, 1987), p. 381.

9. Lewis A. Tambs, "Righting the Dominoes: Democracy, Self-Determination and Ideological Dictators," *New World: A Journal of Latin American Studies* 2 (1987), p. 4. For criticism that the Reagan Doctrine presented the case of Nicaragua to the nation as "an ideological threat" and not as a geostrategic threat, see Christopher Layne, "Requiem for the Reagan Doctrine," *SAIS Review: A Journal of International Affairs* 8, no. 1 (Winter–Spring 1988), p. 7.

10. Josef Kalvoda, "Communist Strategy in Latin America," *Yale Review*, no. 2 (Winter 1965), p. 207.

11. See, e.g., the editorial, "The Weak Position of the United States in its Interamerican Relations," in *Diario Las Americas*, February 22, 1989, p. 4A.

12. Committee of Santa Fe, *Santa Fe II: A Strategy for Latin America in the Nineties* (Washington, D.C.: Council for Inter-American Security, August 13, 1988), pp. 21–22. See also the Committee of Santa Fe's earlier report, *A New Inter-American Policy for the Eighties* (Washington, D.C.: Council for Inter-American Security, 1980), pp. 15–16.

13. U.S. Congress, Senate Committee on the Judiciary, Report prepared for the Subcommittee on Security and Terrorism, *State-Sponsored Terrorism*, 99th Cong., 1st sess., June 1985 (Washington, D.C.: Government Printing Office, 1985), p. 90.

14. Brian Crozier, *Strategy of Survival* (London: Temple Smith, 1978), p. 9.

15. Tambs, "The Reagan Doctrine and Central America," p. 380.

16. Tambs, "The Reagan Doctrine and Central America," pp. 380–81.

Bibliographical Essay

It would be next to impossible to understand the Sandinista movement without reference to its origins in Cuba under the aegis of Fidel Castro, under Marxist-Leninists as Raúl Castro and Che Guevara, and under the Castroite organizer of the Sandinistas, Quintín Pino Machado.

The FSLN (Frente Sandinista de Liberación Nacional), which Pino Machado started in 1960, had been unable to make any headway during the 1960s under its main leader, Carlos Fonseca Amador, the illegitimate son of Don Fausto Amador, a Somoza family manager. Accordingly, there are now ample details on the background of the movement provided by ex-Sandinistas and by veteran journalists. The latter, for example, include journalistic accounts by Georgie Anne Geyer, Shirley Christian, and, in a series of articles written for the *Los Angeles Herald Examiner*, by Merle Linda Wolin in 1985. Among the best of these is Shirley Christian's full-length study, *Nicaragua: Revolution in the Family* (New York: Random House, 1985). As to ex-Sandinistas, see Humberto Belli, *Breaking Faith: The Sandinista Revolution and*

Its Impact on Freedom and Christian Faith in Nicaragua (Westchester, Ill.: Crossway Books, 1985).

As to documentary sources, it is necessary to consult the congressional testimony referred to as the Eastland-Dodd *Hearings* under the heading "Communist Threat to the United States Through the Caribbean" since 1959. Doubtless, the first carefully researched articles based in part on this congressional testimony were written by Josef Kalvoda for *The Yale Review* in 1960 and 1965 under the same title, "Communist Strategy in Latin America." Equally important for the years between the Cuban missile crisis and the beginning of the détente era on Soviet-Cuban policy is the staff study prepared for the Subcommittee on the Judiciary in 1966, entitled *The Tricontinental Conference of African, Asian, and Latin American Peoples*. Some parallels to Soviet policy toward the Third World and in Soviet European policy during these years can also be found in Josef Kalvoda's *Czechoslovakia's Role in Soviet Strategy* (Washington, D.C.: University Press of America, 1978). And on the détente era itself, the reader can usefully consult Chapter 4 of Wolfgang Leonhard, *The Kremlin and the West: A Realistic Approach* (New York: W.W. Norton, 1984), and Chapter 11 of Mikhail Heller and Aleksandr M. Nekrich, *Utopia in Power* (New York: Summit Books, 1986).

Both Castroite and Sandinista ideology and policy have followed Soviet policy and strategy as formulated in 1954 in the aftermath of the abortive attempt to seize power in Guatemala. See in this regard the important study on Guatemala's struggle against communism in *Guatemala: A Case History of Communist Penetration*, Inter-American Series 52, published by the Department of State in April 1957. On the Sandinistas and their re-enactment of the Cuban path to revolution, see also the partial collection of documents included in *The Central American Crisis Reader*, edited by Robert S. Leiken and Barry Rubin (New York: Summit Books, 1987), pp. 148–201. Also, on the façade of adhering to the principles of political pluralism, a mixed economy, and a nonaligned foreign policy, see Douglas W. Payne, *The Democratic Mask: The Consolidation of the Sandinista Revolution* (New York:

Freedom House, 1985), and David Nolan, *The Ideology of the Sandinistas and the Nicaraguan Revolution* (Coral Gables, Fla.: Institute of Interamerican Studies, University of Miami, 1984). Two related questions, which make clear what was at issue from the beginning, concerned the regime's relations with the United States and its attitude toward holding "free elections." As to the former, see Lawrence E. Harrison, "The Confrontation with the Sandinistas: Myth & Realities," *Public Law Review* 6, no. 1 (1987), pp. 25–39. On the question of "free elections" as a means of enhancing the legitimacy of Sandinista rule, the question is really one of electoral fraud. Suffice to say that the subject of free elections is skillfully exploited to disarm the regime's opponents as much as elections are exploited to disarm the Nicaraguan resistance. The FSLN reneged on its original promise to hold elections, despite a poll by Managua's independent daily, *La Prensa*, which showed that 73 percent of the population wanted elections soon after the Revolution. When elections were finally held in November 1984, the outcome was all but foreordained. For FSLN attitudes toward the 1984 election, see Comandante *Bayardo Arce's Secret Speech before the Nicaraguan Socialist Party (PSN)*, Inter-American Series, published by the Department of State in March 1985.

As to the grave social, political, economic, and religious consequences of the Sandinista Revolution, there is much that has been written, both pro and con. Yet overshadowing even these, ultimately, in its seriousness has been the militarization of Nicaraguan society, the massive violations of human rights, and the educational impact of Sandinista policies on Nicaragua. Last are the equally grave foreign policy implications of Sandinista rule on fueling foreign insurgencies and terrorism, and on the creation of a vast refugee flow into neighboring Costa Rica, Honduras, and beyond.

No single source has dealt with all these problems, but a series of publications, governmental and nongovernmental, have attempted to focus on one or another aspect of the issues. Three useful reports that attempt to deal with one or more of these aspects are *Voices Against the State: Nicaraguan Opposition to the FSLN* (The Nicaraguan Research Project), edited by Steven Blakemore (Coral Gables, Fla.: Institute of Interamerican Studies, University of Miami, 1988); *Nicaragua, Civil Liberties, and the Central American Peace Plan* (Washington, D.C.: Puebla Institute, 1988); and Martin Kriele's report, *Nicaragua—America's Bleeding Heart* (Mainz, West Germany: v. Hase & Koehler Verlag, 1985), on the refugee camps in Honduras and Costa Rica.

Equally far-reaching on account of its overall impact on the region has been the FSLN's continued military buildup, its potential for creating social and economic havoc, its external threat to neighboring states, and the serious national security issues posed generally by Sandinista expansionism and aggression. Added to this scene of grave internal and external threats posed by FSLN military power is the influence of the Soviet Union and Cuba, both direct and indirect, on Nicaragua's neighbors.

Studies done on these sets of issues in view of American national security interests and concerns have been reasonably successful. In this vein, see Timothy Ashby, *The Bear in the Back Yard: Moscow's Caribbean Strategy* (Lexington, Mass.: Lexington Books, 1987); Jack Cox, *Requiem in the Tropics; Inside Central America* (Evanston, Ill.: UCA Books, 1987); and Robert F. Turner, *Nicaragua v. United States: A Look at the Facts, Special Report* (Washington, D.C.: Pergamon-Brassey's International Defense Publishers, 1987).

On overall Soviet foreign policy and the response of the Reagan administration, the following should be consulted: Wolfgang Leonhard, "Soviet Foreign Policy: Interests, Motives and Objectives" (May 1983) in H. Sonnenfeldt, ed., *Soviet Politics in the Eighties* (Boulder, Col.: Westview Press, 1984); Lewis A. Tambs and Frank Aker, "Shattering the Vietnam Syndrome: A Scenario for Success in El Salvador," in *Conflict: An International Journal* 4, no. 1 (1983); Mikhail Voskenski, *Nomenklatura: The Soviet Ruling Class* (New York: Doubleday and Co., 1984); and James R. Whelan and F. A. Jaeckle, *The Soviet Assault on America's Southern Flank* (Washington, D.C.: Regnery, 1988). Additionally, see

Central America and the Reagan Doctrine, edited by Walter F. Hahn (Washington, D.C.: U.S. Strategic Institute, 1987), and Lars Schoultz, *National Security and United States Foreign Policy Toward Latin America* (Princeton: Princeton University Press, 1987).

Lastly, as to the social impact of Soviet expansionism, the consequences of Soviet intervention in Nicaragua parallel the earlier consequences of Soviet intervention in Cuba after 1959. In both instances—in fact wherever the Soviets have intervened—the number and flow of refugees fleeing the targeted country has been high. Thus, in thirty years under Castro well over 10 percent of Cuba's population has fled the country, though the percentage of refugees has been even higher in the case of Nicaragua; hence the figure of 700,000 Nicaraguans who have fled their country in the past ten years represents more than one-fourth of Nicaragua's population. Alas, the social consequences of Soviet foreign policy can no longer be viewed as a "secondary" issue by U.S. policymakers as a reason for opposing further Soviet expansionism in the Americas. Rather, the refugee issue must be viewed as a principal reason for opposing such adventurism, if not the most important reason for opposing Soviet intrusion in the Caribbean basin, and in the Americas generally. See in this regard, Lewis A. Tambs, "International Cooperation in Illicit Narcotics and Illegal Immigration—A Grand Illusion?" *Comparative Strategy* 8, no. 1 (February 1989), pp. 11–19. And in the case of Cuba's recent refugees, see Alex Larzelere, *Castro's Ploy—America's Dilemma: The 1980 Cuban Boatlift* (Washington, D.C.: National Defense University Press, 1988).

Index

ABOUT THE AUTHOR

GREGORY WILLIAM SAND holds a Ph.D. in American and modern European history from Saint Louis University. He is currently Adjunct Professor of International Relations in the Master of Arts Program in International Relations at Webster University, St. Louis, Missouri, a position he has held since 1986.

Dr. Sand, who has specialized in U.S.–Soviet relations since 1978–1979, when he began teaching the "Cold War Era," has been aided in his research and teaching in this field through travel grants provided by the Monsanto Fund in 1980 and by the Fritz Thyssen Foundation, which took him to West Berlin and the Europäische Akademie there in 1981.

In addition to editing the Truman-Churchill Correspondence, 1945–1955, a work still in progress, Dr. Sand has embarked on additional projects in this field that he hopes will help to reshape the study and teaching of post–World War II diplomatic history and international relations.